Digital Product Management

Digital Product Management

Design websites and mobile apps
that exceed expectations

Kristofer Layon

New
Riders

VOICES THAT MATTER™

DIGITAL PRODUCT MANAGEMENT
Design websites and mobile apps that exceed expectations

Kristofer Layon

New Riders
www.newriders.com

To report errors, please send a note to errata@peachpit.com

New Riders is an imprint of Peachpit, a division of Pearson Education.

Project Editor: Michael J. Nolan
Development Editor: Margaret Anderson/Stellarvisions
Production Editor: Maureen Forys, Happenstance Type-O-Rama
Copy Editor: Gretchen Dykstra
Indexer: Joy Dean Lee
Proofreader: Jennifer Needham
Cover Designer: Aren Straiger
Illustrator: Adam Turman
Interior Designer: Maureen Forys, Happenstance Type-O-Rama
Compositor: Happenstance Type-O-Rama

ISBN 13: 978-0-321-94797-0
ISBN 10:   0-321-94797-5

9 8 7 6 5 4 3 2 1

Printed and bound in the United States of America

CONTENTS

DEDICATION

For the faculty, the staff, and my classmates in the Department of Design, Housing, and Apparel at the University of Minnesota, where I completed my master's degree in interactive design ten years ago. Thanks for all of the knowledge and, more importantly, the desire and skills to continue learning in the rapidly changing world of digital product design.

Acknowledgements

This is my third time writing a book, and I am just as awestruck and humbled by the process as I was the first two times. And I'm just as indebted to the many fantastic people who make it all possible.

These include Michael Nolan, Margaret Anderson, Glenn Bisignani, Gretchen Dykstra, Charlene Will, Maureen Forys, Aren Straiger, and Jack Lewis. Plus others behind the scenes with whom I did not work directly, but I know helped craft my ideas, words, and sketches into the form that you see here.

Special thanks to Adam Turman, who made this book come alive with his illustrations. Soon after deciding to write it, I knew I had to partner with Adam to help this book be engaging and human centered. So if you find this book to be delightful, it is due to Adam's wonderful graphic contributions.

Also, kudos and thanks to Erin Newkirk and Dan Wick at Red Stamp. Their passion for solving customer problems with new and creative solutions is without peer, and has made their vision for web and mobile products very successful. I'm honored to work with them and to help take the company's product management and UX design efforts to the next level.

I'm also grateful for the many fine people who contributed to my product management knowledge during my previous two and one-half years working at Capella Education Company. Jason Scherschligt, Keith Koch, Rob Kruegel, and Steve Scofield are some of the best mentors I've ever had; they made Capella's Online Products and User Experience department a place where agile, user-centered design leads to new ways of providing online education to people all over the world. And I'm grateful for Capella's mobile team, as well: Matthew Johnson, Kurt Menne, Micaela Vega, Tyssa Erickson, Ashley Alm, Rachel Bowland Ulstad, Todd Anderson, Jessica Chapman, Andrew Barker, Xiaochuan Wang, John Freier, and Priya Gupta. I'm also indebted to my excellent product management colleagues at Capella: Stan Tead, Wade Fields, Rosann Cahill, Thomas Boe, and Chris Pegg.

Finally, thank you to my wife and daughters, who are the most patient and supportive people in my life. Katie, Sarah, Grace, Emma, and Anne: There's no way I can adequately thank you in words for all of the love and joy that you provide.

Foreword

It was 2008 and Garrett Camp's arm was tired. The entrepreneur had spent way too much time trying to hail a cab on the streets of San Francisco. His big idea was to start a limo time-share service. Who wouldn't want to show up to an appointment in style?

Camp saw a clear problem and set out to solve it with a mobile app that lets you order a car anywhere, anytime. Today it's a billion-dollar, multinational business called Uber. Don't know exactly where you are? Your phone's GPS will tell you. Don't have enough cash? Pay and tip automatically with your saved credit card. Don't want to spend the money on a limo? Uber now offers traditional cabs and hybrids at lower rates. Uncomfortable about getting in the car with a stranger? Check the driver's rating before accepting the ride—you'll be required to rate him afterward, and he'll rate you too, improving the experience for everyone.

An Uber driver recently told me that his marriage had been saved by working for the company ("Now I make my own hours, drive a beautiful car, and don't worry about who's getting in my back seat"). Several drivers credit Uber for increasing their earnings by 30 percent.

A great product solves a problem for the buyer and the seller. It might start with a wild idea, but over time it can revolutionize an entire industry and change people's behavior forever.

A great product makes you faster, smarter, stronger, cleaner, or superior in some way. It lets you bring 5,000 of your favorite songs with you everywhere you go, track the exact speed and distance of your morning run, or read an audience's inner thoughts about whatever the conference presenter just said. It helps you quickly shred a block of cheese, perfectly divide an apple into eight equal slices, or remove stains with a magic pen.

Take a moment to look around and count the number of products you use on a daily basis. I stopped counting at 50. Inventions you simply can't live without are everywhere: the living room, the office, the bathroom, the boardroom. All of these places contain the brilliance and hard work of someone who thought something could be done better.

For as long as humans have existed, we've been filling our surroundings with tangible products. Over the last decade, we've been filling our pockets and purses with virtual ones. But one thing is true whether these products are physical or digital: they occupy space. And space is finite. That means every time you decide to bring a new product into your life, you're making the space unavailable for something else.

Consider it: You're as unlikely to put two lamps on your nightstand as you are to wear two activity trackers on your wrist. Products force you to make decisions about what you want, what you need, and what you're willing to spend (in time, money, and effort). You make a sophisticated cost-benefit analysis whenever you consider something new, and many times again for as long as you choose to keep it.

As someone who makes products, your goal is to make the decision to buy and use your creations easy and obvious. And regardless of the industry, form, culture, target audience, or price point, one universal factor will determine your success: purpose.

Purpose is the *why,* the reason something exists, the problem that your product is trying to solve. It's the intended use, the intended benefit, and the intended significance all wrapped into one. Purpose is value—its worthiness to be owned and used. Without intrinsic value, how can you expect your products to stand the test of time?

Product management is the art and science of crafting a product with purpose. It combines the creativity of design with the analytics of business. It crystalizes goals, defines strategy, prioritizes features, focuses design, coordinates development, optimizes testing, and expedites time to market.

So how do you find your purpose? How do you ensure that your products will have value? By not guessing. Wait, isn't all product management a bit of guesswork? That's how a lot of organizations run, but it doesn't have to be that way. The teams behind the most beloved products, physical and digital, share one dominant quality: empathy.

Empathy is the ability to feel the feelings of someone else. Putting yourself in someone else's shoes lets you see the world from her point of view: what she wants, what she needs, what she's willing to spend to make her life better. Developing empathy for your customer lets you create a product she can't live without, not just the product you feel like making.

From Benjamin Franklin to Steve Jobs, the process has always been the same, and so have the blood, sweat, and tears. Know your purpose, understand your customer, and solve the tough problems to make a better world.

WHITNEY HESS
User Experience Coach, Vicarious Partners
www.whitneyhess.com
September 25, 2013

Introduction

As a designer or developer of web or mobile projects, you know the drill pretty well already. You know what I mean—the established, well-intentioned best practices that you make sure to follow as you design, develop, and launch a new site or app:

→ Is it accessible?

→ Does it comply with the client's branding and design guidelines?

→ Does it look great and provide a simple and delightful user experience?

→ Was the writing guided by good web or mobile content strategy?

→ Is the CSS, HTML, JavaScript, or other code modern and standards compliant?

→ If it's a website, is the design adaptive for supporting multiple screen sizes?

→ Has the site or app passed a usability test?

→ Is analytic code in the right places for tracking user behavior?

→ Is there social media integration and a strategy to ensure that people will easily find and engage with the site or app?

→ Are there launch and maintenance plans so that the site or app goes live on time and won't quickly "go stale" after it's released?

These ten points and more should be pretty familiar. They're the subjects of many outstanding books and conference sessions, and, for goodness sakes, you can always get better at doing them, right?

Yet there's a problem: Even if you do all this well, it doesn't ensure success. There's often a significant gap between creative and technical success and true organizational success. This gap is filled by product management.

WHAT IS PRODUCT MANAGEMENT?

In today's landscape of increasingly rapid web and app development cycles, it's not enough to focus solely on project-level attributes for determining success.

In fact, it was never really enough. Success metrics for projects don't completely translate into success metrics for organizations and businesses, for one simple reason:

Most organizations are not in the business of operating websites and apps.

So what do most organizations and businesses do? What are they good at? What do they care about? That's pretty simple, too:

Organizations are in the business of selling products.

Now you might argue that not all organizations are in the business of selling products—I'll cover that in more detail in Chapter 1, "What Is a Product?" But in short, I'll disagree with you here and briefly state that all organizations and businesses sell *something*. Actually, the entire purpose of running any organization or business is selling a product. You just need a broader definition of what selling means and what products really are. Once you have that understanding, it all begins to make sense.

So what does this mean for you as a designer or developer? What it means is that you need to broaden your measures of success. You need to add more criteria to your list that go beyond user interface design, best practices in coding, content strategy, social media strategy, and everything else that designers and developers love to think about, talk about, and implement.

Websites and mobile apps need product management criteria, too. These additional criteria are much more specific to individual organizations and products, but should look something like this:

→ What is your website or mobile app designed to enable customers to accomplish? In other words, are the goals clearly understood and articulated?

→ Do those goals involve delivering content, or do they also involve enabling transactions?

→ How will you verify that delivery and transactions are happening successfully?

→ Who in the organization is interested in knowing the data about delivery and transactions?

→ How will you communicate the data to them, and how often?

→ How do you know that they are the right people to care about customer behavior? Do others in the organization need to know too?

→ What are the measures of success for the delivery or transactions?

→ Do the project's designers and developers understand these measures of success?

→ Does the organization's leadership understand the creative and technical options for achieving that success?

→ Who's managing all of this when everyone is already really busy with their design, development, and management work?

IS PRODUCT MANAGEMENT FOR ME?

You might be thinking that attaching a whole bunch of additional success criteria to your website or mobile app is a bunch of extra work, and that you don't have time for more work. Or maybe you're not a product manager, so you might assume that this extra work falls under that big category of "That Must Be Someone Else's Job."

This book isn't so much about who is or isn't a product manager, and therefore it doesn't focus as much on job descriptions per se (though I do provide a sample job description in Chapter 8, "Getting It Done"), but rather on product management as a category of responsibilities. What's far more important, and what this book spends more time covering, is what product management means to organizations and to design and development teams. My intention is to describe *product* as another way to think about your work that isn't really "extra" at all, but integral to what organizations and teams must be aware of to achieve success.

So is product management for you? Yes it is. Product management will help you be more successful whether you're a designer, a developer, a project manager, a content strategist, or a businessperson. The reason is both complex and simple at the same time: because product management is where design, development, and business are intimately connected. It is where the circles in a Venn diagram overlap—the most important and critical place where creative, technical, and business people need to collaborate and understand one another.

Does this mean that your organization or agency needs a product manager? Perhaps—but again, this book isn't about staffing. Those decisions are up to organizations and agencies. But regardless of whether a single person is assigned to product management work or not, the work is there to be done. This book explains what that work is and how you will know when product management is being done successfully.

CHAPTER 1

What Is a Product?

You might think that because you're working on websites or mobile apps, you're not working on products. Or maybe your clients are nonprofit organizations that don't appear to sell anything at all.

After all, you're probably used to thinking of products as foods, appliances, personal care items, and so on. Products are manufactured. Products are things that you shop for at supermarkets, department stores, or electronics stores. They're things you can hold or set up at home and then use. They're things that help you get stuff done or make your life better.

All of this is true. But step back for a moment and think about what it really means. Are products really just items that come in packages? Are products necessarily sold in stores?

PRODUCTS ARE MADE AND SOLD

When you think about your favorite food, you have something in mind that was either grown or raised by a farmer, or otherwise concocted in a manufacturing facility to be a tangible product (**Figure 1.1**). That item is something that you then purchase in a store or market. As consumers, we typically think of a product as a thing that is branded with a name and available for a price. So there's a creation, or making, process involved in every product, no matter what it is, as well as an acquisition process, a transaction through which you obtain the item so you can use it.

When undertaken effectively, the processes of making and selling should yield a successful product. If the product is not successful, the making and selling processes can be improved. Making these adjustments for quality and success is what we call product management.

So where do designers and developers of websites and apps fit into the product management process? Let's take a look.

FIGURE 1.1 Like many people, one of my favorite product categories is coffee and espresso drinks. My interaction with a coffee shop and its products often involves the company's website or—if they have one—their mobile app. These digital products play a significant role in my overall product experience and, therefore, my satisfaction with the company and what it's selling.

SELLING PRODUCTS INVOLVES EXPERIENCES

Any business exists because it has something to sell. It has a product to sell, or maybe more than one. Perhaps the product is a hard good like a car, or perhaps it's a digital good like an e-book. Or maybe it's a service, such as consulting or education.

The one thing common to all companies—regardless of what they sell—is that they have *something* to sell. And all of these things, when taken together, constitute a vast and diverse marketplace of items and services that compete for consumers' attention.

People understand and experience the marketplace in complicated and sophisticated ways. Buying and using products is about more than just going to a business (in person or online), putting some money on the counter, and walking away with a shiny new product. The world is a competitive place, so there are usually other products like ours. And sometimes products that are not like ours can still appear to be similar.

There are also related products that support primary products. A computer company appears to mostly sell computers, but there's much more to the computer business than selling computers. There are also service plans in case something goes wrong with the hardware, help desk services in the store, and accessories. Service plans, support, and gadgets are also products that computer companies sell to support the computers that they're best known for.

It gets even more nebulous for organizations that are not in the retail space. Take a university, for example (**Figure 1.2**). What, exactly, is being purchased by students when they're completing courses or a degree program? Is it grades? Credits? Competence in applied subject matter? Skills for doing academic research? All of these? These things are all less tangible than the large French roast coffee you might purchase at a coffee shop, yet they're all products of education.

FIGURE 1.2 Higher education is being disrupted by digital technology, which is forcing schools and universities to consider what they're actually selling. Designers and developers are creating new digital products that are part of this evolution of education.

The stores and websites used to sell things are important, too. Anything that requires investment to design and create, involves a customer experience, or impacts a company's success can and should be thought of as a product. It may not be the company's *primary* product and it may even be free.

But that doesn't really matter: When a website or mobile app is designed and built to create a user experience, it's an important part of getting other primary products to market. And it is itself a product whose experience and impact can be managed.

WEBSITES AND APPS ARE ALSO PRODUCTS

If you design or develop websites, mobile apps, or other interactive experiences, you work on an important part of an overall organizational strategy and user experience. It doesn't really matter whether you got into design for the creativity of it, or got into programming because of the precision of it, or got into writing and editing because you like words and grammar. If your work contributes to products, you're also in the business of making sure that your work makes an impact on the success of your organization.

To help make your digital products successful, you'll need to manage them in a way that can demonstrate success and value along the way, from concept to completion. Otherwise, how will you know whether you're working on the right sites or apps? And how will you know whether what you're working on is making any difference in people's lives, in your organization, or in the world?

BE A REFLECTIVE PRACTITIONER

There are plenty of places where the fields of design, development, and writing overlap. And this isn't unique to web or app design. Most jobs blend formal fields of study and practice with other types of work.

If you work in product management, one of your main responsibilities is to bridge these creative, technical, and business gaps across teams and organizations. Product management is a reflective type of practice in which you'll need to examine the impacts of other disciplines, and tell a comprehensive story back to the organization about the success or failure of these collective efforts.

A good book about navigating gaps between fields of practice is Donald Schön's *The Reflective Practitioner* (1983). Schön talks about the nature of knowledge, professional practice, and—more specifically—how problems are solved in work settings. It was a foundational book for my graduate degree in design, and it's remained particularly useful as I've become a more reflective, strategic product designer. One of the main lessons it taught me was how knowledge is discovered and formalized, and how this leads to *disciplines*— approaches for people working in deliberate, systematic, and reflective ways.

Disciplines like medicine, law, and mathematics have existed for centuries; computer science has been around for decades. All of these are ways in which people deliberately, systematically, and reflectively get work done. Reflective practitioners in these disciplines improve their work by doing it slightly differently the next time.

But disciplines like web design, software development, and user experience design are not nearly as established—they've all been created in the past few decades. In fact, they're still in the process of being created. This raises the bar for being even more reflective and adaptive about how we do our work and why. After all, we're not just designing websites and apps for the sake of websites and apps alone.

Schön describes this process of new types of work emerging out of established fields as the inherent tension between technical rationalization and reflection in action.[1] In other words, as disciplines create new ideas and solutions that are disruptive to existing ways of doing things (such as computer scientists, designers, and writers creating the World Wide Web over a period of several years), those source disciplines are no longer adequate to continue guiding this new thing all on their own.

For example, the web involves programming, so it's definitely part computer science. But it's also part design. And the web certainly has a lot of words, so it's part writing and editing. It's all of these things and more. It doesn't just follow the traditional theories and techniques of scientists, mathematicians, artists, and writers.

The web requires new working methods and new ways of thinking. And frankly, it often requires being comfortable with some ambiguity while new ways of working evolve. But as practitioners who wrestle with ambiguity, if we reflect on how we apply familiar ways of doing work and adjust things to develop new approaches, we also create new disciplines along the way.

As new roles of web designer, app developer, content strategist, and online editor continue to take shape, there are also other gaps to fill. The metamorphosis of this hot, sticky mess continues, and one of the gaps to fill is that of making sense of the mess itself. It's a meta-level job, and for websites, apps, and other interactive products, this work is digital product management.

Schön contends that when more established disciplines can't answer all the questions or solve the problems at hand, new disciplines emerge to identify and define new problems to solve.[2] Applying Schön's theory to digital products, web designers may be great at designing layouts and interfaces to solve certain problems. App developers may excel at identifying platforms and frameworks or writing their own code to create functional solutions to other problems. And content strategists and writers can ensure that people are getting the right information, in the right formats, in the right amount, and with enough detail.

But getting all of these people on a team, even with a great project manager, is not necessarily enough. What larger problems is the team trying to solve? And who defines and articulates these problems?

Product management helps ensure that organizations are reflective and deliberate with their design and development resources at a product level and with a product focus. They don't just set out to design and develop something that looks good or is user friendly. A reflective organization connects more dots than that—it seeks to create digital products that meet customers' needs and drive organizational success. By reflecting on their work throughout the design and building processes and confirming value with customers, creative and technical teams can be more successful in deeper and more valuable ways.

Because it doesn't matter how beautiful and usable our websites or apps are. If they don't connect people with organizations or facilitate communications and transactions, then they're not making a difference in people's lives, nor in an organization's accomplishments.

PRODUCT MANAGEMENT CONNECTS CREATIVITY TO BUSINESS

Product management seeks to cover the wide range of territory from strategic organization and business goals to design and development. In doing so, it seeks to fill gaps that aren't adequately filled by the other members of a creative team, and aren't necessarily filled by other members of the business team either. Product management is an important bridge from organizational needs to creative and technical solutions, and it seeks to put digital products into the context of the customers and stakeholders who use them.

But what about *project* management? Don't project managers help to bridge and manage gaps already? They certainly do, and great project managers help drive success by making sure that projects are completed in a timely and affordable manner. However, successful projects do not always result in product success. Let's take a look at how *project* and *product* management relate to each other.

There are a number of great books about project management, a discipline that arose out of the software industry. One such book, *Interactive Project Management* by Nancy Lyons and Meghan Wilker (also known as the Geek Girls), does a great job of helping creative and technical teams leverage their skills to define and complete interactive projects.

In the second chapter of their book, the Geek Girls draw a parallel between an interactive project team and an orchestra (**Figure 1.3**). They use a diagram that illustrates their contention that the project manager is the conductor, and the other team members comprise the orchestra. [3] I think this analogy is both brilliant and accurate: Interactive projects do require an interdisciplinary team. Like an orchestra, an interactive team can't be successful if everyone plays the same instrument. When a great orchestra has a great conductor, the result is great performances.

FIGURE 1.3 Nancy Lyons and Meghan Wilker compare an interactive team making digital projects to an orchestra playing a symphony.

But, extending their analogy, who writes the music for the orchestra? And who selects the compositions to form a concert program? And who researches and compiles dozens of compositions from a variety of composers or genres to construct a full orchestra season of several concert programs?

Managing something as a product is comparable to creating concert programs and annual subscription series for an orchestra. Like the conductor, the *project manager* is essential for the individual compositions (projects) to be carried out successfully.

But just as the artistic director of a musical organization researches and creates music programs to meet the interests and tastes of its patrons, a *product manager* researches and creates product definitions and strategies that meet the needs of a business organization's customers (**Figure 1.4**). And just as an annual concert series provides the framework for individual orchestra concert events, product management strategies and road maps provide direction for individual projects that will enhance digital products.

> **NOTE** Imagine an orchestra that plays with technical and artistic perfection but regularly performs music that its audience does not like. In this case, the excellent performance of the music will not result in success, because the music does not match audience tastes. Digital product management seeks to diminish similar risks in website and app delivery by having customer expectations drive creative and technical projects.

FIGURE 1.4 A concert program is both a collection of music selected by the orchestra's creative director—product manager—and a physical or digital representation of that music program that is used to market the event ahead of time and make the event experience better.

So with that, welcome to the world of web and mobile products, and welcome to product management. Because whether you're a full-time product manager or are taking on a few aspects of product management in addition to your primary role on your team, the work of product management is there to be done. This book will help you better understand what that means: how web and app products can be designed more deliberately, and how their success can be measured more comprehensively.

SUMMARY

Chapter One covered two basic questions: What is a product? And what is product management? Here are some highlights:

→ A product is a good or service that is designed and developed to meet the needs of an organization's customers.

→ Some products are sold and some are free. But even free products solve market needs by facilitating purchasing or other transactions involving primary products. A good example of this type of sales product is a store, a designed experience for facilitating sales transactions of other primary products.

→ Successful products delight customers, earn a profit, or help organizations meet other strategic goals. Products should be developed with all of these factors in mind.

→ Product management helps to ensure that websites and mobile apps not only successfully meet creative and technical goals, but also are held accountable for their business impacts and user satisfaction.

→ Product management is a highly reflective practice, in that it connects creative and technical disciplines as well as business and management practices. The goal of product management is exceeding customer expectations. This requires awareness and assessment of how websites and mobile apps impact the way people interact with organizations.

→ Interactive projects are put into better perspective and context with product management. When considered separately, individual projects can improve specific product features or services. But from a product point of view, projects are seen as an iterative series of enhancements that add customer and organizational value.

→ Product value can be measured in terms of customer satisfaction and organizational success; it can be used to continually improve the strategy of the organization as well as the ongoing work of creative and technical teams.

REFERENCES

1. Schön, Donald. 1987. *The Reflective Practitioner: How Professionals Think in Action*, 39. Jossey-Bass.

2. Schön, 40.

3. Lyons, Nancy, and Meghan Wilker. 2012. *Interactive Project Management*, 17. New Riders.

CHAPTER 2

Understanding Markets and Customer Expectations

In Chapter 1, we established that digital products such as websites and mobile apps should be designed and developed in a way that meets the needs of the organization's customers. This was probably not earth-shattering news: no matter what your role in interactive work, you most likely already wanted to deliver something that people like to use.

But when I mentioned markets, you might have started to wonder whether this book is for you. Fear not: understanding markets and customer expectations does not require you to wear a tie and become a business expert.

Every businessperson should understand markets and customers. And while you may not always think of yourself this way, designers, developers, content strategists, and project managers are all *businesspeople*. Helping other team members understand markets and customers is a central responsibility of product management.

The better you understand markets and the expectations of the people you're doing work for (both external and internal customers alike), the more successful your work will be.

And that's good business.

MARKETS AND DEMAND

We've all seen houses for sale where the real estate agent's sign is in the yard for a really long time—sometimes for months, sometimes for a year or more (**Figure 2.1**). The place just isn't selling, even though it seems to be a perfectly normal house.

What does this mean? Can the house really be that bad? Why won't someone finally buy that thing, anyway?

FIGURE 2.1 Many forces play into whether something sells and at what price. It's not about what the seller thinks—it's about what the buyer thinks. This is the impact of markets, and customer demands and expectations.

If the owner is your neighbor, you might get into in a conversation that sounds something like this:

You: "Hey, too bad about your house. It's been on the market for a while, hasn't it?"

Neighbor: "Yeah, it sure has. I'm starting to get impatient! It's too bad, because people don't know what they're missing.

You: "Oh?"

Neighbor: "Absolutely. My house is fantastic! I've poured my heart and soul into this place and spent a fortune making it better over the past several years."

You: "It's a shame that people aren't seeing that. I know how much you've done with it. It looks good to me."

Neighbor: "The crazy thing is, I've had several people come through and say they love it. They compliment every aspect of it. But later they tell my agent that they think I've listed it for too much. Can you believe it?! Why aren't they willing to pay me a fair amount for all of my hard work and investment?"

You: "Huh, pretty crazy. That's too bad!"

On the surface, such a story sounds unfortunate for the seller. Why don't people see how much work and investment have gone into something? If people say they like something, why aren't they buying what they like?

The trouble with a scenario like this is that the seller, who's explaining about all of the hard work and pricey investments that have gone into the house, is really just making an emotional appeal about the home's value. The seller acts as if the hard work and generous investments automatically result in high value for a buyer.

But that's not how it works. In this example, value to a prospective buyer isn't determined by what the homeowner has done to the house, nor is it determined by how much money the work cost or how much time it took to get the work done. Value for the buyer is not controlled by the homeowner. Rather, value is in the eye of the beholder—the customer. She either likes what she sees or she doesn't, and either thinks it's worth the asking price or it isn't.

CUSTOMERS DEFINE VALUE

Value is determined by customers and what they like or need. In the above example, what customers like or need determines whether there is market demand for the home.

 A pink bathroom or a living room with brown and orange carpeting might be your idea of heaven. But unless you find someone else who has the same taste, you'll have a hard time selling your house because, unfortunately, the market for your house might be only one person: you (and you can't sell it to yourself!).

Indeed, to successfully sell a home, you need a market of at least one like-minded person—hopefully many more. You need to find people who appreciate the same things you do, and ideally people who value those things as much as you do. If you do, you can probably find someone to buy your house for what you think it's worth (leaving aside the ups and downs of the real estate market for the moment).

But even if you find other people who share your interests and tastes, you're still in a bind if their interests and tastes aren't as strong as yours. The degree to which a potential buyer likes what you do determines what she's willing to pay: If she likes it as much as you, you're in luck because she might value it highly. But if she doesn't feel as strongly as you, she might value it only half as much as you. Or less. Your opinion doesn't matter.

Similarly, as a designer, developer, writer, or project manager, it's important for you to think about market demand, because it doesn't matter what you think about a site's design or code. I hate to say it, but it's true—your opinion just doesn't matter that much when it comes to determining the actual value of what you're developing. And it doesn't matter whether you think the content is fantastic, or whether you've delivered the work on time and on budget, either.

Many of these things might matter internally to your organization, of course, but they don't necessarily matter in the same ways to the customers who use the digital products. You can't channel your personal investments and passionate preferences into your customers and make them think that your work is great just because it took a lot of work, you love the results, or it was built on time and on budget.

How much you love your own work, or how much effort it took, is immaterial in terms of its actual market value. The rest of the world has needs and desires, and your sites and apps need to meet those expectations.

They need to meet market demands. Customers determine value.

MARKETS AND SUPPLY

Markets don't just run on customer demand, however. The equal and opposite factor is supply.

Let's revisit the example about selling a home. Recall that the buyer shopping for a house will buy one only if she really likes it. And she'll only pay your asking price if she likes the house as much as you do. If she likes it, but likes it less than you, she'll probably try to negotiate the price lower. After all, if she doesn't feel as strongly about it as you do, she'll be more willing to walk away if she can't get a good deal.

But what if she really loves your house—and another house in a nearby neighborhood, plus another house a few miles away. In fact, this buyer loves several houses.

Welcome to the law of supply and demand. Even if the buyer really likes your house, if the supply of similar houses is large, the demand for a particular house on the market goes down. With many other options available, the buyer simply doesn't need to pay top dollar for a specific house. The supply gives her more flexibility to negotiate the price down or walk away.

So as you're determining what market problems you're trying to solve for your organization's customers with a website or mobile app, be aware of other options that address the same problems. Be aware of your competition.

Answer the following questions:

→ If there are other organizations similar to yours, what are their websites or mobile apps like? Are their sites or apps like yours?

→ If your product is too similar to others, what can you do to distinguish your product from the competition? Should the distinction be content, design, performance, or features (or all)?

→ If your competition is known to update their product often, how does your product compete with that? Do you try to match the pace? Can you?

→ Is your organization or client placing too many expectations on a site or app, and paying too little attention to how the core business is being competitive?

→ Are there other ways to help your organization be successful besides the website or mobile apps?

If you're like me, you've already taken the time to look at comparable websites before embarking on your own work. But this is about much more than generating ideas. It's about making sure that, as a design and technical team, you're aware of what similar organizations are doing with their websites and mobile apps. You want to work that knowledge into your data arsenal, and highlight places where being similar is advantageous but where being different could even be more advantageous.

NOTE | **Being aware of the competition ensures that when a client or supervisor asks you about something the competition is doing, you're not taken by surprise. As a designer or developer, your credibility to clients and businesses is a valuable asset.**

Spend time nurturing your market credibility by regularly doing market reconnaissance, and communicating the findings of your competitive analysis in ways that are easily understood by those you're trying to inform. Use Harvey Ball diagrams to compare details of different products (**Figure 2.2**). You can highlight whether a feature or capability is available, only partially available (or successful), or missing (or unverifiable).

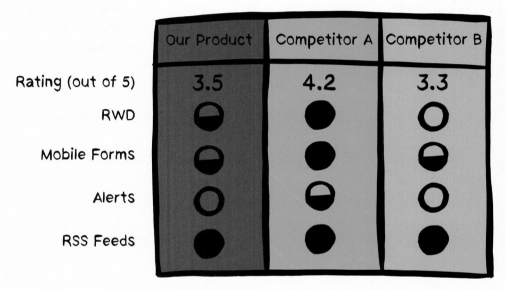

FIGURE 2.2 A Harvey Ball diagram compares features and capabilities between similar competing products. The diagram also includes a comparison of ratings on a five-point scale. You can make a persuasive argument for prioritizing the design and development of enhancements by comparing features in this way and correlating them with ratings.

WHO IS A CUSTOMER?

As useful as competitive analysis is, when it comes to markets, studying your competitor's products is only the beginning of an adequate understanding. It's more important to study your customers themselves. And by study, I mean interact with them—however you can.

But first, as a product team, you need to recognize that you have internal customers and external customers. And they might not be looking for the exact same things.

Internal customers

Internal customers—executive leaders, marketing directors, other departmental directors, customer service people, and others who work directly with external customers—will see the role of the business or your product through the lens of their personal responsibilities. That might seem a bit weird at first, but it sure is helpful.

 Remember, each of us sees things through the unique lenses of our experience and areas of focus or expertise. Designers tend to see sites and apps through the lenses of functionality, beauty, logic, hierarchy, and the like. Developers see them through the lenses of code and performance.

Business executives might not have a great "design eye" or might not care about the code running behind the scenes, but they will care about what it costs to create and maintain the site, and about the results of that expenditure.

Fortunately, bridging the gap with a businessperson is fairly easy to start: Arrange a meeting or give her a call, and begin to develop a relationship.

This might sound kind of obvious. But in practice, for most designers and developers, it is not. We generally choose to forge relationships with people who are most like us. This is perfectly natural, but it's not beneficial to the products we work on.

The best thing you can do for your site or app is to understand what makes your internal customers tick. What are their most important responsibilities, and which of those can be supported by a website or app? Designing and developing sites and apps that don't impact the top priorities and strategies of an organization's leadership is probably not a good use of your time.

External customers

Even more important are your interactions with external customers, or users of your site or app. There are as many ways to interact with external customers as there are types of businesses and types of customers, which means that there is no single right way. But there are several options:

→ Create an online survey and ask customers to tell you about their product expectations and priorities.

→ Identify customers who are willing to take a survey over the phone. Even hearing inflections in comments can provide valuable insights into their opinions.

→ Best yet, invest some time in meeting with customers, even if it's only a few people. Interview them, brainstorm with them, or have them look at a prototype—or even just a current site or app—prior to any enhancement. Get their opinions, whatever it takes.

If you need help connecting with customers and gathering their insights, check out Steve Krug's book *Rocket Surgery Made Easy.* It isn't really about rockets or surgery, but rather usability testing. I highly recommend it, and, as you read it, be sure to read between the lines. There's a lot more to the book than learning how to discern usability problems in an existing digital product. At its core the book is about understanding customer expectations and how to meet them.

FOCUSING ON MARKET PROBLEMS

You're probably quite familiar with usability testing for an existing product or working prototype. However, to discern measures of success for a new product or product feature, you need to conduct testing at an earlier point in the product life cycle. If asking people about a nonexistent product or feature sounds hard, think again.

It's not so much about getting people to imagine using something that isn't yet real, it's about getting them to articulate problems that exist—problems that your site or app should solve. These are *market problems.*

Focusing on market problems is the right way to proceed with design. Remember the example of the house that won't sell. The problem with that scenario is that the house pleases you, but it doesn't please any of the prospective buyers—the customers. It doesn't matter how much the house pleases you when it comes to selling. If the house doesn't solve any market problems, it won't appeal to anyone who's in the market for a new house. And it won't sell.

Determining market problems and then focusing on them is a much smarter way to design. It helps keep your personal biases as a designer or developer in check. It's not that your experience, creativity, and technical expertise don't count—they certainly do. But true design is problem solving that serves other people, whereas creating something that primarily pleases yourself is a hobby. (There's nothing wrong with a hobby—the whole point of a hobby is to entertain or please yourself.)

So don't be a design or development hobbyist. Focus on solving real, confirmed market problems. And solve them in a way that distinguishes your organization or clients from others. If you solve the right market problem with the right solution, your products can be incredibly successful!

SUMMARY

What's most important to know when you're designing or developing a website or mobile app?

→ It's important to understand markets, or the forces that result from everyday people having problems that need solutions. Solving a problem in a creative and affordable way can lead to great success.

→ Conversely, biasing your creative or technical work toward what you value personally can be very risky if what you like doesn't align with market expectations.

→ Understanding market problems involves talking with real people, either in person or on the phone. A more convenient alternative that can still collect meaningful market data is an online survey (but nothing beats real face-to-face communication).

→ There are two kinds of customers: internal and external. Understanding them both is equally important, as a successful business meets both internal and external expectations.

CHAPTER 3

Writing User Stories

Having a solid understanding of market problems and customer expectations is the foundation of good digital product management. With that foundation, you can take the next step: shaping the information into goals that will guide the work of design and development teams.

The best way to accomplish this is by writing user stories. User stories are concise, simple statements that describe how or why people expect to use a website or mobile app. But despite being written for design and development teams, these statements are written in human terms and focus on everyday problems. And as you learn more about writing them, you'll come to understand why this is very important.

There are some general principles for creating user stories, and a few key elements that distinguish great user stories from good ones. Let's cover some principles first.

PRINCIPLES OF CREATING USER STORIES

User stories have essential aspects that make them different from other writing that may be part of product design and management workflows, such as business requirements or technical specifications.

Write in the first person

This might seem a bit silly or unimportant, but it isn't trivial at all. At its essence, a user story is intended to get designers, developers, business analysts, executives, and others into the mindset of the customer.

User stories have a rather serious element of role-playing to them: You're trying your best to understand what your customers need. So you don't want any distance between their role and yours, and therefore you don't want any "us and them" language. The user story needs to take you out of your regular work role and put you in the role of your customer.

So the wording should always be something like this:

 As a customer of Company A, I am able to...

By starting this way, a user story tells you who you are and what you're trying to do. It helps you see through the eyes of your customers and better understand their lives and how your organization is trying to serve them (**Figure 3.1**).

When you understand your customers and what they need, you can do a better job of meeting their needs—and hopefully exceeding them!

Use everyday language

A good user story uses simple language. There are two reasons for this.

First, the user story is the starting point and ongoing reference for all aspects of creating or enhancing a website or mobile app. Many different people might be involved in the conversation about the product and refer to the user story, including customers, business owners or stakeholders, designers and developers, and others. To facilitate their understanding of the story, use everyday language. People often get confused or sidetracked by creative or technical terminology. While such terms might be very important parts of conversations within teams, it's best to avoid them in conversations between product teams and others.

FIGURE 3.1 User stories help to humanize the tasks and needs that you're being asked to solve. Over time, user stories and customer feedback bring you closer to people and their everyday lives.

Second, everyday language should represent what people need to accomplish via their encounters with your digital product. True, some digital products, such as games, are destinations unto themselves. But most websites and mobile apps are designed to solve a particular problem or communicate something specific. Therefore, user stories must focus on those goals in a very clear and concise way. When they do, they help everyone involved in the product stay focused on people.

Avoid creative or technical solutions

One of the biggest risks to user stories is creative or technical creep. No, I'm not insulting your creative or technical staff—I would never call them creeps. What I'm saying is, as you begin to think about things to design and build, it's easy to get excited about your ideas. And you can quickly get wrapped up in how you want to solve your customers' problems. Too often, as soon as you start writing down the problems you're trying to solve, your writing starts to include possible solutions.

This is bad, at least in the context of user stories. User stories should be free of creative and technical solutions. They need to remain pure and focus on human, nontechnical goals.

The range of possible technological solutions may expand and contract as creative and technical team members wrestle with how to solve a problem. And this is all natural. But notes and details about creative and technical solutions should go elsewhere in project documentation. (I'll leave those approaches to project management, design, and development books. There are many out there if you want to read about how to manage design and development processes.)

Focus on generic, fundamental goals

The final principle of user story writing is that it should focus on general and timeless goals. Try to make the user story one that is enduring and as safe from platform and technology changes as possible. You want the user story to have a long shelf life and not become outdated, and you don't want changing contexts on the solution side to inadvertently impact how you think about the definition of the customer's problem.

As an example, see if you can identify the problems in this user story:

 As a user of the XYZ iOS app, you need to be able to get your registration data into the SquishySoft database with your iPhone.

Here's what's wrong:

1. XYZ iOS app: At the very beginning, this user story includes a specific product name (XYZ) and a third-party product platform (iOS). You may want to think twice about using a specific, customer-facing product name in your user stories if the name could change. And you may not want to constrain your solution thinking to iOS—that's a technical solution detail that doesn't belong in a user story.

2. "You" and "your": Hey, I thought I said you have to write user stories in the first person! Right. Well, it's easy to forget that sometimes. Always use "I," "my," and "mine" to help pull yourself into the situation.

3. Registration data: Real customers never talk like this! Avoid using words like "data" in a user story—that's a technical term. Most customers use "information" or refer to specific data types, such as "my address."

4. **SquishySoft database:** If your customers don't use the word "data," they sure aren't going to be talking about your database either. Again, every time you insert something specific and, especially, backend related in a user story, you constrain the team's thinking. What if this enhancement should consider another database solution? Or is there another way to capture the data? This level of detail just doesn't belong in a user story.

5. **iPhone:** Using a specific device type like iPhone may or may not be appropriate in your user story. Are you specifically managing an iPhone-only app? If so, this is probably OK, although it could change in the future. If you're managing a broader mobile solution that can or could be on more than one platform, referencing an iPhone is too specific. Again, it keeps discussions and solutions too constrained.

A more appropriate way to write the important needs in this story might be like this:

 As a customer of Company One, I need to be able to provide my home address to the company via my smartphone.

This is a user story that complies much better with the basic principles we've discussed so far. It's written in the first person and focuses on a customer's needs with respect to the organization, the wording is nontechnical and is free of jargon and specific solution-based terminology, and the details specify what the customer is trying to provide (home address) and how (via smartphone).

The various aspects of the user story are generic, as this transaction type will always involve an address. And, for the foreseeable future, this person will want to be able to do it on a smartphone, even if his preferred smartphone changes (**Figure 3.2**).

FIGURE 3.2 A user story written about a customer needing to provide his address to a company via a mobile device should focus on the bare essentials of the problem being solved: The company needs the address, and the customer prefers to submit via a smartphone.

THREE ELEMENTS OF A GREAT USER STORY

Now that you know the basics of writing a user story, it's time to learn how to write *great* user stories.

A great user story is actually about more than describing a user's problem in everyday, nontechnical terms. A great user story also encompasses some success measures.

Success measures? You mean a user story should lead to not just a solution, but a *successful* solution?

That's right, you formerly idealistic designer or developer! You can no longer just dream your way to a proposed solution that loosely fits to an abstract user story. Now that you're interested in managing your website or app as a product, you need to think about its business or organizational success. And you can define the success right inside that handy little user story.

Do this by focusing not just on the desired output, but also the related outcome and impact. So let's see how all of this works.

Output

Incorporating the output of a user story is pretty straightforward. The output describes what a customer expects to accomplish on your site, that is, the transaction or interaction itself, and in basic rather than technical terms. Here are some examples:

 As a user of Website A, I am able to sign up for an event...

and

 As a user of Mobile App B, I can get help from a librarian...

In these examples, registering for an event or getting help from a librarian are the essential tasks that the user wants or needs to complete. They are, at their most basic, nontechnical tasks, which makes the tasks the basic elements, or output, of the product.

In most cases, you should be able to verify that the output of a user story is basic and nontechnical by determining whether the task or event exists offline. Ask yourself whether the customer could do the same thing without using a website or app. In these examples, there are indeed other ways to register for events or get help from librarians—these things were being done for centuries before websites and apps came along. So they pass the test as being basic outputs of the solutions being sought in the user story.

Outcome

Adding an outcome to a user story is also pretty simple. An outcome describes what the user hopes to accomplish by completing a task in your web or mobile product:

 As a user of Website A, I am able to sign up for an event by completing a reservation process...

or

 As a user of Mobile App B, I can get help from a librarian so that I can learn the right format for citing a source in my research paper...

In these examples, signing up for an event or contacting a librarian are important tasks, and we now know why they're important: The tasks enable the user to get something else done, reach a goal, or understand a process.

When measuring the success of a design, you want to not only track the outputs, but also, if possible, the outcomes of the outputs. That's why including the outcomes in your user stories keeps your team and organization focused on what really matters: helping people do things in order to meet their goals.

Impact

There's one more component for making a user story not just good, but great. Try to incorporate the impact of the user story being solved, the impact on the organization or the client who is commissioning the work. Why do they care whether a user can do something to meet a goal? If they care and there's a reason, it should be included in the user story:

 As a user of Website A, I am able to sign up for an event by completing a reservation process, which will make me more likely to attend the event.

or

 As a user of Mobile App B, I can get help from a librarian so that I can learn the right format for citing a source in my research paper, which will make my paper comply with my school's citation standard, resulting in a higher grade.

The fact of the matter is, your organization isn't interested in designing a new solution for users just to be charitable. No matter how kind your leadership is, there has to be a more concrete reason why they're investing in a feature, capability, or product enhancement. Include that reason in the user story. This is actually the most important thing to measure—the ultimate impact of your work.

The impacts of these user story examples are decidedly nontechnical and noncreative. Attending an event isn't a web thing—it's showing up at an event in person. That's measured by counting bodies in the room.

And having papers comply with a standard isn't particularly technical either. Papers either comply with a citation standard or they don't. The measure of success is counting the papers that comply. Or counting the number of passing grades that result from the papers being formatted correctly.

Writing good, complete user stories that include outputs, outcomes, and impacts keeps meaningful goals visible for the product team, the organization's leadership, and the customers themselves. And if the team refers to the user stories regularly and always keeps them in mind, the goals stay visible throughout the entire process of user experience analysis, design, development, and then measuring ultimate success.

Keeping everyone's attention focused on the real human or organizational problems being solved, and the real human or organizational goals that are accomplished as a result of the work, is the best way to approach product design. It forces the team to stay focused on what matters most: people and their lives.

SUMMARY

This chapter explained why user stories are essential to digital product management and how to write them well:

→ Use a first-person perspective. A user story is intended to pull you into the mindset of the customer and what he's trying to do.

→ Write user stories using everyday, nontechnical language so that the meaning is clear and focused on customer and organizational needs.

→ Don't let creative or technical solutions creep into user stories. Keep them focused exclusively on clearly articulating problems or issues. That's their sole purpose.

→ Keep user stories timeless. Avoid references to platforms, other products, or anything that's likely to come and go. Use the broadest possible concepts to keep options open and to maximize flexibility and creative potential.

→ Clearly state an output in every user story: What does the customer need to do?

→ Clearly state an outcome in every user story: What desired result does the customer get from the task?

→ Clearly state an impact in every user story: Why does the client or organization care about the customer having this outcome? The answer to that question is what helps define the ultimate value of your product team's work.

CHAPTER 4

Analyzing and Prioritizing Enhancements

Chapter 3 explained how to write user stories about new product features or ways to enhance existing products. If your product team spends time doing this and accumulates a list of user stories for enhancing a product, you'll end up with a backlog of ideas.

Defining a bunch of issues to solve begets yet another problem: How do you decide what to work on? Unless you're in a very unusual situation, you have limited time and budget. There are only so many hours in a day, and only so many people to work on design and development.

Of course, one of the most difficult things in life is prioritizing. It's just a universal problem, isn't it? If you haven't done this well, it seems you're always making excuses and apologizing.

"Sorry, I don't have time!"

"I'd love to help you with that, but I just don't think I'll be able to."

"Argh, I'm too busy!"

"What do you mean I need to get that done by next week? I'm already booked up! THERE'S NO WAY I'M GETTING THAT DONE BY NEXT WEEK!"

While you can't add days to the week, you can learn to manage your time more effectively. This chapter will help you think about priorities that make sense and then set up a structure that will enable you to stick to them.

Once you have a structure and prioritization habits that you can trust, there will be fewer apologies. And if you do still have to apologize occasionally for not getting everything done, you'll have clear reasons to give for why other tasks took priority, and this will hopefully cause less anguish and stress. You'll be more confident in setting and meeting user story priorities, and letting other things fall to the wayside or deferring them until later.

So let's see what this looks like! We'll focus on two frameworks for analyzing priorities: Maslow's hierarchy of human needs and the Kano Model.

MASLOW'S HIERARCHY OF HUMAN NEEDS

Abraham Maslow (1908–1970) was an American psychologist (**Figure 4.1**). In 1943, he wrote an article for a professional journal, *Psychological Review,* called "A Theory of Human Motivation." I remember first learning about Maslow and his theory in college, thinking that a hierarchy of needs seemed quite logical. And after getting into product management work, I think it's an even more powerful idea. So let's spend some time going over his theory and how it applies to product work.

FIGURE 4.1 Psychologist Abraham Maslow was best known for his theory about the hierarchy of human needs.

What first interested me about Maslow's work was the fact that his research centered on healthy people rather than sick people. I found this inspiring and uplifting, because in popular culture we seem to encounter more examples of the opposite: psychology and its medical counterpart, psychiatry, as sciences that deal with human mental disorders and how to manage or "cure" them.

Maslow's career itself represents a way of working that creative and technical people should learn from. His theories and research were not just extensions of ideas and work of colleagues whom he agreed with. Rather, Maslow questioned the status quo of psychology and developed alternate understandings of how people work and why they do what they do.

Sound familiar? It's kind of the basis of product management: seeking a greater understanding of people and then aligning your work with that understanding, rather than going with generally accepted practices and broad, industry-wide understandings. The best creative and technical solutions are the result of asking hard questions, digging deeply, and finding new answers that can lead to new ideas—answers for specific, real customers, not just answers that align with general trends that may or may not align with your specific market.

Maslow's work provides a useful way to think about how people function and, especially, what distinguishes humans from other species. Essentially, what makes humans unique is our capacity for self-determination and our ability to work through priorities. Humans make choices about a lot of things, and Maslow believes there's a system or hierarchy to how we make these choices.

Understanding this hierarchy can help you better meet people's expectations with your products.

Here are the five levels of human needs that Maslow identified (**Figure 4.2**):

1. **Physiological needs:** Our basic needs include respiration, food, water, rest, getting rid of waste, and reproduction. Without these basics, we can't survive as individuals, nor could we carry on as a species.

2. **Safety needs:** These needs include bodily security, moral security, and mental security. If you're hungry and have food, you'll eat and take care of that immediate need. But then how do you get more food for tomorrow? Your next meal becomes a bodily security issue.

3. **Social needs:** These needs are about emotional stability and happiness. They include friendship, family, and intimacy.

4. **Esteem needs:** These needs involve broader external acceptance that leads to greater self-esteem and confidence. You might be well fed, know where your next meal is coming from, and feel happy and loved. But until you're secure and confident in your education and employment, for example, your happiness is limited to a fairly small sphere of existence. Esteem gives you the confidence to live outside your comfort zone.

5. **Self-actualizing needs:** These high-level needs—such as morality, creativity, and problem solving—are what distinguish us from other species. Some people succeed in these areas more than others, and because of this we have a broader spectrum of humanity: good people, bad people, people with vision who can make the world better, and people who are shortsighted and selfish.

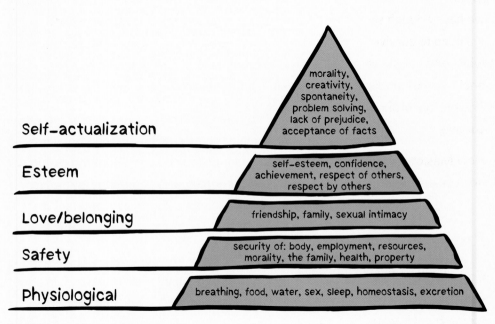

FIGURE 4.2 Maslow's hierarchy of human needs. Basic needs—those essential for survival—are at the bottom. Higher-level needs are at the top.

You have to meet the needs at the lowest level before you can advance to the higher levels. It's hard to satisfy broader security concerns if you're not breathing, eating, and otherwise healthy!

There's a lot of analysis we could get into at this point. For example, why do good people sometimes do bad things? I think Maslow's theory actually speaks to this. Most of us would never steal from others in a normal situation, because we have enough security in our lives to know where we'll be getting the things we need to survive from day to day. But seeing this hierarchy of needs explains why good people could be forced to steal if their circumstances were bad enough. This is why looting sometimes happens in times of war or civil unrest: The normal order of things is upset, and people can devolve a bit in order to survive.

How Maslow's hierarchy of needs applies to product design and development, however, is where it gets really interesting for us.

Product-level hierarchies

Consider how digital products dovetail with Maslow's hierarchy of needs. For example, why is Google one of the most-visited websites in the world? The hierarchy of human needs tells us why: Google can help us meet many of our needs, even fundamental ones. We use it to find food, to get answers to our health care questions, and to buy diapers.

We even use sites like Match.com to help us find lifelong partners with whom, should it interest us, we can start a family!

So it's little wonder that Google and other search engines have become ubiquitous in the developed world. People would be pretty lost these days without them, especially on their mobile devices. Sure, there are tons of apps out there, and we frequently download new ones, but often we'll give them a try once or twice then stop using them because they fail to meet our fundamental needs. But have you ever heard of anyone saying, "Yeah, I got tired of some of my apps and got rid of a few, and I decided to give up using search this time. Who needs it?"

Uh, no. No one has ever said that. Ever.

After search, online banking websites and mobile apps are probably among the most-used digital products. Why? Because they help us meet our safety needs—they enable us to get paid and, in turn, to pay the bills for goods and services that keep us safe, secure, and comfortable.

Think about where your current websites or mobile apps fit into Maslow's hierarchy of needs. Do they support the base of the pyramid, a higher but less critical level of needs, or a range of needs? Knowing this should help you set expectations for use and satisfaction.

Similarly, if you're assessing a new product opportunity for a client or trying to discern what kind of site or app to design on your own, determine what type of needs it could meet. Could it satisfy fundamental needs or higher-level needs? Could it be used by a broad range of users or just a niche?

Attribute-level hierarchies

There's a more nuanced way to look at hierarchies of needs: looking at specific product attributes, features, or capabilities. What does this type of analysis look like?

After Maslow's theory caught my attention and I saw how relevant it was to product management in general, I started thinking about how I could modify it specifically for online products. What are the online equivalents of our physiological, safety, social, esteem, and self-actualizing needs?

I came up with my own version of Maslow's hierarchy, applying it to mobile user experiences (**Figure 4.3**):

1. **Physiological needs:** When making the web work on a mobile device, the physiological equivalent of breathing and eating is seeing and navigating. In other words, nothing else really matters until you can see it and go from one part of it to another. These are the most basic aspects of online content.

2. **Safety needs:** These needs are related to repeated or sustained activity. Eating is great, but where's your next meal coming from? Seeing and navigating is one thing, but reading is another. Reading is a deeper, more sustained activity that involves the most pervasive form of online content: text. Seeing text is a good start, but having it sized, scaled, and formatted in a way that makes it clearly legible is even better.

3. **Social needs:** These needs include engagement with content through responding and sharing. Not surprisingly, the web excels at both with elements like forms and social media. As you prioritize web optimization for mobile, solve visibility first, readability next, and then make sure that people are able to respond and share with mobile-friendly forms and social media connections.

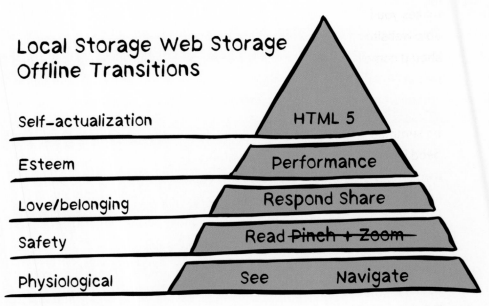

FIGURE 4.3 My theory of mobile motivation. Like Maslow's hierarchy of human needs, it illustrates that there are basic needs to meet in mobile user experience before higher needs can be met. This isn't specific to mobile user experience; people accessing content and interactions in desktop or tablet browsers have the same needs.

4. **Esteem needs:** On the web, one of the best sources of confidence and trust is performance. How many of us have experienced a site or service that is designed well but plagued by downtime or sluggish performance? (Remember Twitter's infamous "fail whale"?) It can be very discouraging to see a site with a great, practical design, but then be let down by the service being sporadic or unavailable. It not only cheapens the site, it makes you feel unimportant as well. And this feeling isn't trivial; if a reliable website or app can empower you to do something better or faster, it should come as no surprise that something you can't trust can make you feel powerless and insignificant.

5. **Self-actualizing needs:** The final tier of needs for digital products can be summed up with one word: joy. And for a great example of this, we need look no further than the first iPhone. Phone calls, texting, maps, e-mail, cameras, and the web already existed, of course, but the iPhone combined them in one device in a truly elegant and pain-free way. Apple later added an app store to enable people to design nearly anything else that they wished. In short, the iPhone created joy—not a fleeting, giddy feeling of happiness, but rather an enduring level of product satisfaction that has made it the best-selling phone (and camera) ever.

I like how this hierarchy of web and mobile needs works out. And my friend Brad Frost liked it, too. He boiled it down into the simple diagram shown in **Figure 4.4**.

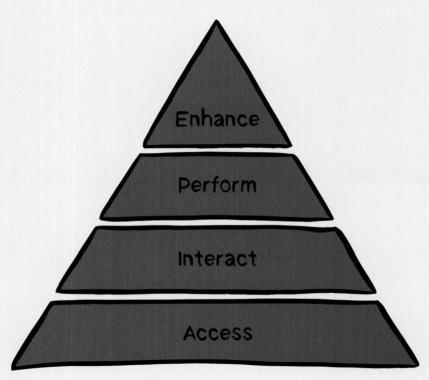

FIGURE 4.4 Brad Frost's diagram of mobile needs: access, interact, perform, enhance.

The importance of support

For me, the worst product experience—no matter what type of product or service it is—is not having a simple way to contact the company for support or to complain. Acknowledging customers as people means giving them a means to communicate with you, confirming that their messages are received, and responding to their inquiries.

Don't underestimate the importance of providing a customer support channel for your website or mobile app, even if it's just an e-mail address. And if it's an e-mail address, be sure to check the in-box regularly and write back to the people who contact you, even if it's just to thank them for reaching out. You'll earn their trust and increase their satisfaction, even if your initial reply doesn't solve their problem.

What I like most about his interpretation is that it shows that the hierarchy is flexible. And that's kind of the point. As long as your priorities are based on customer needs and market problems, your approach to websites and mobile apps can vary slightly. Just make sure that you're careful when you prioritize, and structure the needs in a way that enables you to meet essential ones first, then others later.

This brings us to the Kano Model, a systematic way to think about any product attribute and place it in proper perspective.

THE KANO MODEL

The Kano Model is named after Noriaki Kano (born 1940), an educator and writer who taught for several decades at the Tokyo University of Science (**Figure 4.5**). He spent much of his career in the 1970s and 1980s developing and fine-tuning an approach to analyzing customer satisfaction. The essence of his approach is that all product attributes are not equal to customers, and therefore improving each product attribute doesn't necessarily result in higher customer satisfaction.[1]

FIGURE 4.5 Noriaki Kano, a researcher and educator in the field of quality management, developed a model of customer satisfaction that uses concepts similar to Maslow's hierarchy of human needs. But his model articulates them even more specifically to the work of managing products and customer satisfaction.

Well, that can't be right! Why wouldn't improving something result in more satisfaction? Better is better, right?

Not exactly. And Kano's model of analyzing product attributes explains why. It's similar to Maslow's hierarchy of human needs, but instead of five levels, it has three broader categories of product attributes: basic, performance, and delightful.

Basic attributes

Basic attributes are exactly what they sound like: basic, assumed, fundamental. They're absolutely essential to the product. If a basic attribute is missing, the product doesn't work. Basic attributes are usually pretty easy to confirm in physical products. For example, if a flashlight didn't have a switch, it would be impossible to turn it on or off. Therefore, a switch is a basic product attribute of a flashlight.

Performance attributes

Performance attributes are less binary than basic ones, and therefore can be delivered across a range of performance or effectiveness. A switch on a flashlight is either there or it's not—you can't *kind of* have a switch. Furthermore, even when it's there, a flashlight switch doesn't have much room for improvement. It's going to turn something on or off regardless, as long as it's functional.

But a performance attribute of a flashlight is the brightness of the lightbulb. A strong bulb could result in higher customer satisfaction, whereas a dim bulb could result in lower customer satisfaction. There's a range of brightness associated with lightbulbs.

Delightful attributes

These attributes, sometimes called excitement attributes, are not as broadly anticipated or assumed by customers. And they're definitely not a core expectation. With a flashlight, a delightful attribute could be the color or material of the handle, or even something as subtle as the texture of the grip that you hold on to. Such details aren't absolutely essential, as the flashlight is designed to shed light on things. But the right color flashlight, or one that's easier to hold on to, could be more delightful to use.

So these are the three product attribute categories of the Kano Model. But we're just getting started. It gets more interesting!

Different attributes, different results

The Kano Model category names themselves provide some clues to understanding them. Let's look at a few corollaries to the Kano Model.

Missing basic attributes are a product's biggest problem, but delivering them results in low satisfaction

This doesn't seem very fair, but it's true. Consider a car, the industry that Kano originally based much of his theory on. There are hundreds of different cars that are designed and manufactured by different automotive companies, but they all share some product attributes, one of them being a steering wheel (**Figure 4.6**). All cars have them. So do trucks and minivans. It doesn't matter what the body type or passenger capacity is, all cars have steering wheels. They're a basic product attribute of a car.

FIGURE 4.6 A steering wheel is expected and necessary for a car to work, so it's a basic Kano product attribute.

Without a steering wheel, the car is incomplete.

What's interesting, though, is that providing a steering wheel in your car doesn't garner you much praise, if any at all. Customers just aren't going to pat you on the back and say, "Awesome feature! I love the steering wheel!" No. While a steering wheel is necessary, providing it doesn't result in high product satisfaction. It only results in adequate satisfaction.

But leaving the steering wheel out of the product does quite the opposite. It results in very low product satisfaction. A missing basic expectation means that you haven't just underperformed, you've failed. Selling a car without a steering wheel is indeed failure. The car won't work and isn't safe without a steering wheel. It's an incomplete product.

Performance attributes are often customer specific

The most important thing to recognize about performance attributes is that they're not nearly as universal as basic attributes. A missing steering wheel is a missing steering wheel—there's just not much to debate there, no matter who the customer is. So the universality of a product attribute can be a clue as to whether it is basic and expected.

 NOTE Performance can be in the eye of the beholder. What kind of performance? There can be several kinds!

Going back to the automobile example, consider a common measure of performance for cars: speed. If speed is your measure of performance, it might lead you to buy a sports car, one that goes from 0 to 60 mph in just a few seconds and has the agility you need to zip around those other cars with much more sluggish performance (sounds kind of fun, doesn't it?).

But this definition of performance isn't necessarily for everyone, at least when it comes to purchasing a new car. You might like a fast car, but depending on who you are and what you can afford, you might not actually buy one.

So consider alternative interpretations of performance, such as fuel efficiency (**Figure 4.7**). It's somewhat the opposite of a sports car, which favors speed over fuel efficiency. But for many people who are more conscious of expenses and environmental impacts, owning a car with the best fuel efficiency is the measure of great performance. For them, getting more miles per gallon of gas is another way of defining high performance.

FIGURE 4.7 Fuel economy is something with a linear range of performance, from low to high, making it a performance Kano product attribute.

Additionally, how about seats or cargo space? If you're the parent of multiple children, you're probably not looking to buy a sports car. And you may be less interested in fuel economy than a single person who has the luxury of maximizing fuel efficiency by driving a really tiny car. To you, performance may have another definition: How many of your children and their friends can fit in the vehicle? And how much of their gear can it haul? Or how many bags of groceries can it carry?

Delivering performance or delightful attributes doesn't compensate for missing basic attributes

Think again about a car without a steering wheel, an example of an incomplete product. If you're the product manager for this car, you could have your engineering team vastly improve the fuel efficiency. Or fine-tune the design of the interior to increase the amount of room for passengers or cargo. You could even sell a version with a convertible roof (**Figure 4.8**). That would be especially delightful, right?

But with this example, it's easy to see that improving the car's performance or adding delightful attributes won't make up for missing a basic feature. A car with great fuel economy and a convertible roof won't do you much good if it has no steering wheel. A nonfunctional car is a nonfunctional car, regardless of the additional features it might have.

When prioritizing enhancements on a digital product, make sure that you never diminish the importance of a missing or flawed basic feature. And never make the mistake of thinking that enhancing another area of the site or app will make it easier for customers to accept the missing or flawed feature. Unfortunately, I've heard that argument all too often: "Well, we can't really address that problem right now… but doing this other enhancement should help in the meantime, and give them something else to be happy about."

That's not how it works.

If a basic feature is missing or broken, it's missing or broken. Don't think you can distract customers with a bunch of other improvements. You'll just squander their goodwill and reduce product satisfaction. If you roll out an enhancement that doesn't resolve another, more pressing issue, customers won't be any happier. And any positive reaction to the new enhancement won't be nearly as strong later, either.

FIGURE 4.8 A convertible roof on a car isn't essential, nor does it enhance the car's performance. It's an option that can make driving the car really fun in sunny weather, so it's a delightful Kano product attribute.

Performance and delightful enhancements are effective only when the context is an otherwise complete product. Poorly timed releases of performance and delightful features are at risk not only for not increasing product satisfaction, but also for deepening customers' doubt in your product and its ongoing management and development.

Today's performance or delightful feature can quickly become tomorrow's basic feature

One of the biggest challenges with digital products is customers' rapidly changing expectations. Consider how quickly expectations evolved after the introduction of the iPhone in 2007. Certainly, mobile phone owners' expectations didn't shift immediately; after all, even today many people haven't upgraded to a smartphone of one kind or another. But when people do, the flexibility and usefulness of the device can really get them hooked.

Just this week, I saw some interesting changed expectations in action as they relate to smartphones. As I'm writing this, it is the last week of May 2013. Yahoo just announced a new, updated design of its Flickr photo service. It's really nice, so it got a lot of positive reviews and press.

But in the midst of the positive attention was a significant amount of backlash and criticism, too. Why? The Flickr redesign didn't include an updated mobile-optimized version of the site. And given how influential apps like Instagram have been, and even Twitter with its inline photo display, an updated Flickr design that impacts only desktop users seems rather quaint and less significant than it would have been in the past. And for people who browse the web primarily on their smartphones, the updated Flickr is not just a nonissue, it's also a bit insulting.

Clearly, expectations for digital photo sites have changed rapidly due to widespread smartphone adoption and competition from sites like Instagram. So don't rest on your laurels: Don't assume that because you have a popular digital product today, you'll have continued smooth sailing tomorrow. Expectations for your website or mobile app will change. It's just a matter of when.

Will you be paying attention, doing industry research, and staying in touch with your customers to know when it happens?

Visualizing Kano attributes

Let's take a look at a standard Kano product attribute graph, which makes it a bit easier to see how different product attributes relate to one another (**Figure 4.9**).

As you can see, the red line depicting basic features does just what was described earlier. When a basic feature is delivered, the line plateaus slightly above zero on the y-axis of customer satisfaction to indicate that this generates feelings of adequacy, not hearty pats on the back.

But also note how steeply the red curve dives to deep dissatisfaction when delivery of basic attributes doesn't happen and execution is poor. Poor execution of an expected feature results in very harsh feelings: anger, frustration, sadness. People can feel very strongly about a broken product. Don't let that happen with your digital product.

The green line, representing performance attributes, is linear. That's because poor delivery results in less satisfaction, and good delivery results in higher satisfaction. It's easiest and most predictable to improve performance of a site or app however you can, whether it's speed, ease of use, or some other measure. Any attribute that offers a range of options or examples can fall into this category.

Customer Satisfaction

Quality of Execution

"what a surprise! Great work!"

"Very nice. Much faster than the previous version."

"I don't even expect that."

"Of course. So what?"

"This isn't as good as I expected."

Basic – Assumed, expected features
Performance – Standard features
Delight – Exciting features

"Terrible! This is broken."

FIGURE 4.9 As shown in the Kano Model, customer satisfaction and dissatisfaction vary greatly depending on the quality of basic, performance, or delightful features. Understanding these differences and relationships is key to successfully influencing customer satisfaction with product management decisions.

Determining Kano attributes

Analyzing a car to determine that a steering wheel is basic, fuel economy is performance, and a convertible roof is delightful is pretty straightforward. But what about determining Kano attribute types for a new or enhanced product where you're not yet certain which features would be considered basic, performance, or delightful by your customers?

In their book *Universal Methods of Design*, Bella Martin and Bruce Hanington explain that you can ask two questions of your customers, and their answers to these questions can help you categorize features according to the Kano Model.[2] First, ask how they would feel if your site or app had the feature in question: satisfied, neutral, or dissatisfied. Then, ask how they would feel if that feature were not there: satisfied, neutral, or dissatisfied.

Here's how their responses map to Kano product attributes:

Basic: The customer would be neutral about the feature being there, but very dissatisfied if it were missing.

Performance: The customer would be satisfied if the feature were there, but dissatisfied if it were missing.

Delightful: The customer would be satisfied if the feature were there, but neutral if it were missing.

Remember that if you're verifying a performance feature, having a follow-up conversation about how well or how much of a feature is there and having that map to less or more satisfaction (versus a more binary response) also confirms that it's a performance feature.

Finally, the blue line charts the range of customer reactions to delightful attributes. Because they are unexpected, a missing or poorly executed delightful feature does not usually result in poor customer satisfaction. Customers either aren't expecting it or won't feel terrible if it's there but not perfect. It's an extra, so not a big deal.

But a very well-executed, delightful feature can take your product into the highest stratosphere of customer satisfaction. So the blue graph goes the highest on the y-axis and is essentially the reverse trend of a basic attribute graph.

Charting your product attributes, whether existing or planned, can help you see whether you're focusing on the right user stories at the right time. If you have an expected attribute that's faring poorly in customer satisfaction, don't let yourself get distracted by performance or delightful attributes. Use this graph with team members, executives, or clients to help make this message clearer.

SUMMARY

Chapter 4 explained how to analyze and prioritize product attributes. The most important things to remember are the following:

➜ Maslow's hierarchy of human needs helps you understand what people need the most and how meeting needs is progressive.

➜ Maslow's hierarchy of human needs can help you set priorities for digital products. For example, people need to access (see and navigate) content and services above all. Next in importance is readability, followed by the ability to interact, and then performance and other enhancements.

➜ The Kano Model uses three categories to analyze customer satisfaction: basic, performance, and delightful.

➜ Delivering basic product attributes doesn't earn you accolades, but not delivering them results in severe customer dissatisfaction.

➜ Performance attributes are linear: The better (or more) you deliver, the higher customer satisfaction is.

➜ Delightful attributes are the opposite of expected ones. Not delivering them doesn't result in much customer dissatisfaction (because the attributes are not expected), but delivering them can surprise and delight customers, which can result in high satisfaction.

➜ Don't neglect basic attributes in favor of performance or delightful ones. No performance or delightful feature will make up for a missing basic attribute.

➜ Expectations can change rapidly: Today's delightful feature can be tomorrow's performance feature and next year's basic feature.

REFERENCES

1. Martin, Bella, and Bruce Hanington. 2012. *Universal Methods of Design,* 106. Rockport Publishers.

2. Martin and Hanington, 107.

CHAPTER 5

Completing Minimum Viable Products

Now that you've written your user stories and prioritized your work, do you just dig in on design and development? Is the rest of the process just like it's always been; that is, do you write requirements and come up with comprehensive designs, then do a lot of work as best you can and hope it all tests well with users when you're done?

That's certainly the traditional way of doing a project: creating the best possible design and plan, then executing the plan as thoroughly as is practical, hopefully also working as quickly as possible and therefore making the project as affordable as possible.

Maximizing the planning and estimating before any work begins is what's known as a *waterfall* approach. While this approach may seem responsible and forward thinking, there's inherent risk in trying to define a large amount of work up front, get all the details right, and then develop and test from start to finish. Basically, the more work you try to do at once, the longer and more complex the path is from start to finish. So the odds are higher that things will go differently than you expect.

The waterfall approach isn't inherently bad. But there's a less risky way of getting things done.

A product management approach focuses on smaller batches of work. You break up proposed improvements into bite-sized chunks, test and validate each chunk with users before building too much, and complete the work on each chunk as best you can. The team repeats this process over and over, one step at a time.

In order to do this, you need to get comfortable with the idea of completing less work and releasing fewer results to your customers at once. You need to embrace the idea of a *minimum viable product* (MVP).

WHAT IS AN MVP?

As Jeff Gothelf notes in his book *Lean UX*, MVPs don't have to refer to actual product releases to customers. They can be defined as internal milestones of various kinds (**Figure 5.1**).[1]

 NOTE Don't be misled by the word *minimum* in the name. It might conjure up negative connotations—a lazy team expending minimum effort. This isn't about minimum thought or attention, but rather the minimum amount of change to make, test, and validate the next improvement or design idea.

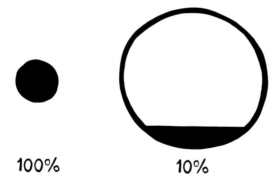

100%   10%

FIGURE 5.1 The basic idea behind an MVP is to define a small amount of work that you can complete, rather than struggle with a larger amount of work that never gets completed. It's better to get 100 percent done of 10 percent than to get only 10 percent done of 100 percent.

You're considering a larger product and selecting a small part of it to work on. At a minimum, the enhancement needs to fulfill some testable function. And at a minimum, the enhancement should result in more product feedback for you. So it's about quantity or degree of completeness, not quality. Quality is still maximized—that's the top goal.

The word *viable* is equally important. Think about what *viable* means: feasible, possible, attainable, and, above all else, capable of working successfully. Something can't be viable and fail or be mediocre. An MVP isn't the most meager version of something you want to accomplish. It's actually the smallest amount of success, with the requirement for success being nonnegotiable.

Gothelf also explains that the core purpose of an MVP isn't to get measurable work done on a product or to achieve a product that's releasable. Rather, the purpose is to learn something significant and to help prove what's true about your team's design ideas or hypotheses. In other words, as he puts it, MVPs are for running experiments.[2]

Let's consider a few different forms of MVPs and how and when your web or mobile team can use them.

Whiteboarding

You might be thinking that sketching on a whiteboard and sharing your crudest ideas with customers or project stakeholders is risky and even unprofessional. Hardly. It's one of the most important things you can do to provide them with more value.

Whiteboarding an idea with a few customers in the room is a great way to start collecting data about a proposed product enhancement or new feature. And when you think about the investment—an hour or two and some dry-erase markers—it's clearly a very low-waste example of an MVP. Remember, the point of an MVP is to maximize product value (viable) with the least amount of work needed to achieve that value (minimum).

Prototyping

The next level of an MVP for your design and development work is prototyping. There will be certain details that you just can't verify very well on a whiteboard, so some level of prototyping will help.

Informal prototyping

The simplest, most affordable, and least wasteful method of prototyping is to use paper. Small index cards are great representations of smartphones and large ones are reasonable representations of small tablets.

Paper prototyping is a great way to take sketching to the next level. With a stack of cards, some markers, and some sticky notes, you can simulate a variety of designs and even start getting into user interface interactions. Plus, it's a way to help the user comfortably participate in design: Anyone can sketch, so if he has an idea in mind based on your initial suggestions, his input can potentially take your idea much further than you expected (**Figure 5.2**).

FIGURE 5.2 You can learn a surprising amount from low-fidelity prototypes sketched on paper. They're the best way to work through ideas quickly before anyone else sees them, and yet they're also great for the first round of validating ideas with customers and clients.

Paper prototyping can result in a great MVP. The resulting artifacts, while very informal in nature, can end up representing some great paths forward for the team—paths that can help engage everyone from designers to developers, as design nuances and technical feasibilities are then further explored. This can also result in the next round of MVP: a more formal prototype on a device.

Formal prototyping

There are many different ways to create realistic-looking and -behaving prototypes that work in web browsers and on mobile devices, and there are many software options as well. I've seen beautifully rendered designs with realistically simulated buttons and screen transitions convincingly created with animations. And then there's the full range of prototyping software that creates everything from rough prototypes that appear hand-drawn to finished products.

What you use will be determined by your budget, and also by how your team prefers to present ideas and get feedback at different phases during the product design and development cycle. But you should be aware of the trade-offs that come with more formal, higher-fidelity prototypes.

A more detailed prototype can give the customer or stakeholder a more realistic depiction of what he'll encounter in the released product. On the other hand, it also makes the design and user experience (UX) appear to be more complete. Some people react to that by offering fewer critiques, as it appears that the opportunity to influence the design has already passed. Don't underestimate this tendency! Also, realize that telling people it only looks done but isn't *really* done doesn't always help. When something looks done, it looks done. We tend to believe what we see.

But the most obvious risk in creating a formal prototype is the amount of time required to make one. Putting something together on a whiteboard or note cards is a snap compared to creating a lifelike prototype in presentation software. Even a tool that's designed to make prototyping faster isn't as speedy as sketching. Plus, just as the more formal prototype tends to make the user think it's more done, you and your team will do the same. The more work it takes to make the prototype, the higher your investment and the less likely you'll be to change it.

So use more formal and higher-fidelity prototypes only after you've done plenty of informal prototyping and are finished working through a lot of options and decisions. If a question you have about a proposed solution can be answered with an informal prototype, stick with that and don't move on to a more formal version simply to make it look better. The point of a prototype is never to look good, it's to communicate ideas for the purpose of additional experimentation.

In short, make formal prototypes only when you want to

→ Explore design and interaction details that truly require that level of prototyping during idea discovery and validation with users.

→ Document and demonstrate design and interaction patterns for designers and developers.

→ Prove hypotheses or solve problems that can't be solved with lower-fidelity, informal prototypes.

Sometimes even a formal prototype isn't sufficient for what you're trying to prove. And that's OK—it just means you're moving along the prototyping spectrum and have reached the need to start coding a solution.

Partially built feature

When your team is finished prototyping and ready to begin building an actual feature, remember that you don't have to finish, test, and release a complete solution to production. There are baby steps along this path. You can just build a partial feature.

It's important to remain both skeptical and open-minded as you journey from idea to launch. This can be difficult to do, because as you validate rough design ideas and then start to confirm more details and actual interactions, it's natural to gain confidence and feel more certain about your proposed solution.

But don't let confidence and certainty set in too deeply. You could still encounter some feedback along the way that could alter your direction. If you do and you think it's significant, don't feel dismayed. Changing course in response to learning something new doesn't mean you're taking a step backward. After all, it's better than having to redo something that's fully complete, right?

Released feature

Finally, you think you have something "done enough" to be released. Badge unlocked! Mission accomplished! You've arrived! Right?

Of course, it's natural and healthy to want to celebrate a completed feature or redesign when you release it to users. You have to determine when something is viable, otherwise your tendency toward perfectionism will get in the way and you'll never feel confident enough to put your work out there to be used.

As the product manager, you'll determine whether enough work has been completed to release a feature to users. This makes sense—you discovered the market needs from customers or business colleagues, wrote the user stories to document those needs, and set the team's work in motion to define solutions.

It makes sense, then, that you're in the best position to decide when it's time to release. You have the context to know when something feels right for production and is ready to be in public view. Furthermore, you have the big responsibility of representing the customer. Rereading their user stories, you have to honestly state, "As a customer, I'd like to…" and then follow up by using the feature and asking yourself, "OK, can I really do that now, and am I satisfied with the experience of doing so?"

If you can answer yes to that question, you've just completed acceptance testing for the project. This phase of the product is ready to be used. And you're done! Well, at least until you learn more about your work and there's something else to tweak, adjust, or improve—because a product is never really done, right?

GETTING FEEDBACK ABOUT AN MVP

Now that you know about different kinds of prototypes and the reasons for using them, you need to know how to get feedback from users. Prototyping isn't just a navel-gazing exercise for team members to visualize how something will work. It has to be more than that—as long as you have something to see, you may as well have other people see it, too, and invite them to tell you what they think.

So what are some ways to do this? Let's take a look.

Speaking informally with users

The easiest way to get feedback from users is to sit down with them and just talk. Show them a sketch or a paper prototype, or do a whiteboarding session with them. Or invite a user or two to sit in on a similar activity with your team. This interaction doesn't even have to be formalized to the point of calling it usability testing, if that helps you do it. Just call it a "Chat with Joe" or "Discuss enhancement with Meghan" when putting it on your calendar.

 NOTE | **Getting in the habit of showing people ideas earlier and more often can be hard, because it feels like you're exposing too much to people. I think part of this is the art legacy of design. We grow up thinking that all creative people have studios where they do their work, and therefore great work must be done behind the scenes.**

There's no doubt that in order to get some good work done, it's often helpful to sequester yourself somewhere. For example, when I write books I do most of my work quietly and alone at the library, away from my home and my regular office. It's perfectly normal to want to minimize distractions and be able to focus.

But don't let that mentality lead you to think that all aspects of creativity and progress need to be secretive. Talking about your work regularly with customers can give you a lot of confidence that you're on the right track, which reduces risk and increases the likelihood of success later.

Make a habit of getting people together and talking one on one or in small groups, or having them listen in on a team discussion. Do this as often as you can, even if it's with the same few individuals. As they get to know you better, they'll be less likely to withhold information—they'll get past that awkward "first date" phase of trying to be overly polite and cautious, and not wanting to offend you.

In the end you want your users to feel that they know you well enough to say whatever is on their minds.

Surveying

Another informal way to get some great information from customers, especially those you can't meet with in person, is surveying them online. All you need is a mailing list and a surveying tool such as SurveyMonkey or Vovici. It also helps to reference a whiteboarding session that everyone attended, or to provide a link to an online prototype.

It's amazing how much you can learn from a short survey. In ten questions or less, you can glean a ton of information about customer preferences and priorities. Furthermore, by scaling to more than just a handful of people, online surveying can give you more confidence (it might not be statistically significant, but that's OK).

Here are a few tips for surveying customers:

1. If you want to know specific information, don't be shy about writing specific questions. Sometimes you need to be really focused with people in order to get the information you want.

2. However, if you're in an earlier phase of getting information about an idea, being too specific might constrain your options too much. This is especially true when dealing with a new category of features or content where there are a number of options. This means there are a number of places where your team could begin its work.

In this case, ask the survey participants about the broad idea and try to get specific answers (for example, "Do you like food?"), but as a follow-up also give them an open-ended question (like "Please tell me your two or three favorite foods"). For the second type of question, just giving them a list of a few items to choose from may exclude too many possibilities. Instead, provide an open text field where they can enter their own ideas. This will result in a wider range of feedback.

3. Strive for no more than four questions per screen (depending on the type), and no more than four screens of questions. That way each screen doesn't take too long to complete, and each screen completed shows up as the survey being another 25 percent complete.

4. Be sure to thank everyone who completes your survey with an e-mail, usually a few days after the deadline you set for completion. This is also a great way to remind anyone who did not complete it to do so. To accommodate the procrastinators, be sure to set a deadline a day or two before you really need all the data. That allows you to collect those last few responses. And they aren't always insignificant; I've seen the number of results go up 10 percent or more on the last day!

5. Share the data from your surveys with anyone and everyone. The data from surveys is invaluable in being able to cite what customers really want, so do this whenever you can. Your customers' opinions are always more important than your own.

By representing your customers' preferences, you'll encounter less resistance when trying to lobby for a product enhancement or improvement. It's much harder to argue with your actual customers—the people who are truly paying everyone's salaries—than it is to argue with a single team member's opinion!

Card sorting

Card sorting is a fantastic method for doing exactly what the name implies: sorting through a bunch of ideas or options and trying to make more sense of them.

Card sorting is pretty straightforward. You can use actual note cards with one idea or feature on each of them, or use a web tool like Trello to do the same thing (**Figure 5.3**). Trello has a nice drag-and-drop interface that makes it really easy to sort the cards, and all you need to do for user participation is to provide them with a guest account or screen share the app on the web.

Traditionally, there are a couple of use cases for doing a card sort:

1. **Prioritizing**: If you have a bunch of user story ideas within a category (for example, different types of notifications that you'd like your iOS and Android apps to send to your customers), then a card sort can really help you prioritize the items in the category.

   If your team or company executives have dreamed up a list of ten or more notification types, but you only want to begin delivering a few, how do you set the priority? Having users sort them can be a big help. And if you have enough users do the same card sort, you should start to see some patterns that will help you feel confident about where to begin.

2. **Grouping**: Another useful way to leverage card sorting is to help make sense of a bunch of items by grouping them. A great example of this is gathering customer input for designing navigation. Sometimes using an alphabetical ordering of items is a logical approach to grouping items. But when it isn't, then what?

FIGURE 5.3 Card sorting can help provide structure for a large number of items that may not fall into obvious, logical categories or order. Having users sort and suggest ways to order or group always teaches you something you wouldn't see on your own.

Then you have to find another systematic way to order or group items, and often the best way to do this is to go directly to your customers. This not only increases the odds that they'll see things in the places they expect to, but it also helps with the nuance of naming navigational items. Sometimes what you choose to call something internally is not meaningful to customers, so they can help you make better word choices along the way as they both sort and critique the items on your cards.

In-person usability testing

Sitting down with actual customers and watching them use an MVP right in front of you—whether it's an informal prototype, a formal prototype, or a partially built feature—is very informative. Never underestimate the value of doing this in person, even with just a few people, on a regular basis.

Seeing people use things in person reveals a bunch of additional information, some of which is subtle, yet it's all valuable. Consider all the subtle information present in people's tone of voice, body language, facial expressions, and whether they hesitate or not before moving ahead with an interaction. There are countless things to observe and react to. That's what makes in-person usability testing a goldmine of product feedback.

Be sure to balance your approach as you guide these sessions. Work with a seasoned UX or usability team member if you can, and be sure to include other team members. Referring to the Lean UX approach once again, Gothelf emphasizes the benefits to everyone of being with actual customers using your actual work. A good usability report can be excellent, but seeing people use your prototypes in person is more direct and unfiltered, and can yield a variety of possible conclusions that result in healthy design discussions later.

However, this does require a considerable investment in either bringing people to your office to test in person or traveling to meet them at home, at work, or elsewhere.

Online usability testing

The next best thing to seeing customers use your prototype in person is seeing them use it online. Depending on whether it's a website or mobile app, and how you've made the prototype, there are various approaches to conducting usability testing remotely and online.

In terms of reducing waste, online usability testing is *better* than in-person testing. Just like sharing (or screen sharing) documents or sites in online meeting rooms for work collaboration, there are options for sharing (or screen sharing) prototypes online. That way if the users you've recruited to test are far flung you can still do usability testing. Consider the value of being able to test with an international customer base!

When you do usability testing online, try to do as many of the same things (and in the same way) as you would in person. Don't let yourself think that doing it online is any "less real." Treat the process, as much as possible, as you would when doing the testing on-site by using tools that let you record the results or let other team members join the process online.

Ultimately, what you learn from online usability testing is only as valuable as your faith in the process and your enthusiasm for the results. So, as with any product management practice, do your part to amplify the value of online usability testing to the rest of your team and to your organization's leadership. Because even if obtained remotely via an online experience, the results of user testing can be just as valuable as any other method of customer feedback.

Lab-based usability testing

Sometimes it's worth the extra effort to do a lab-based usability evaluation of a product. There are a number of reasons for this. One is that the additional formality of the process often results in better and more detailed preparedness by the team. You develop a test script with more care, invest more in selecting participants, and plan ahead for when it all happens. Formality begets more formality, and that can have its advantages.

Of course, the drawback to all of this is that if you use an actual usability lab, you're probably paying for it unless your company has its own lab space and equipment. That can cost quite a bit. Also, you should engage a professional usability tester to facilitate the process.

Another issue is frequency of user testing. It's probably unlikely that your team can swing formal usability testing every month, and maybe not even every quarter. It may be quite infrequent. And this infrequency can also boost investment and scope (you tend to want to test more if you're testing less often).

If you can afford it, the results of lab-based usability testing can be very worthwhile. Plus, using a lab and some professional help can, as most consulting situations do, add gravitas to the results. And it's hard to beat the power of gravitas for emphasizing test outcomes, as it's always better to have backup for your own conclusions.

In the end, however, don't ever let a lack of formal, lab-based usability testing stress you out. Be content with informal usability testing if that's a better use of your resources. Only go the route of formal usability testing when time and budget permit, and you think the extra layer of formality, rigor, and number of tests you do is truly called for.

NOTE | For more about usability testing, I can't recommend Steve Krug's book *Rocket Surgery Made Easy* highly enough. It's a concise, entertaining read about testing and related topics, and it details the process and expectations from beginning to end. Most importantly, Krug acknowledges the value of more frequent, less formal testing and then offers approaches and advice for carrying it out.

SUMMARY

Chapter 5 explored some important aspects of the iterative product design process, namely how to prototype ideas in a bite-sized manner and ways to get customer feedback along the way to validate proposed solutions:

→ Always think about your work in terms of minimum viable products (MVPs). At any given stage of design and development, what's the least amount of work that can be completed and done well in order to test a design hypothesis?

→ At the earliest stages of UX design, determine whether whiteboarding or showing a simple paper prototype is enough to demonstrate an idea and get user and stakeholder feedback. If so, stick with these approaches and iterate on the basic idea with these methods as much as possible.

→ If you progress to the point that sketching on a whiteboard or testing with paper prototypes is no longer adequate, it's probably time to start building more sophisticated prototypes using computer-based prototyping tools. Still, keep the prototypes as simple as possible. You can learn a lot from an informal prototype.

→ Don't move to formal prototypes until you really need to start validating design details and specific interactions. And sometimes a formal prototype isn't even needed; use your judgment!

→ Finally, start building as little of the real solution as possible in code (remember: MVP) and continue validating with users and stakeholders as often as you can. Continue on the path of incremental, yet continually validated, work to minimize risk.

→ Use a mix of informal conversations, card sorting, surveys, in-person usability testing, and online usability testing for most of your data and opinion gathering from customers. Use lab-based, formal usability testing sparingly—it's expensive, and it saves you work more than it yields more accurate usability findings.

REFERENCES

1. Gothelf, Jeff. 2013. *Lean UX,* 56. O'Reilly Media.

2. Gothelf, 56.

CHAPTER 6

Measuring Success

You now have some techniques to help validate product enhancement ideas early and often, and you know the path to getting a product improvement prototyped, designed, developed, and launched into production.

That must mean you're done, right?

Not so fast.

Getting a new (or enhanced) product into the hands of your customers merely means that you've finished one phase and are ready to embark on another. And this new phase is one of the most critical in product management: measuring success.

But remember, measuring success isn't just about embedding some analytics code into your site or app, sitting back, and collecting data (**Figure 6.1**). That's a key part of the effort, to be sure. But it's really just scratching the surface.

If analytics is just the beginning, what else does measuring success involve? Let's take a look.

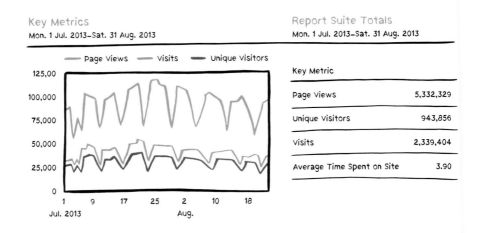

FIGURE 6.1 Web or mobile analytics can give you great data about the use (output) of your digital product. But that's just the starting point: What are these interactions truly enabling your customers and organization to accomplish?

RETURN TO YOUR USER STORIES

The first step in measuring success is to return to your user stories. Remember those?

> ## User stories: the most essential elements of product management
>
> Here's why: After you think you've solved the issues defined in your user stories, you need to refer back to them to see how successful you were. And you do that by checking out the three key elements that comprise them: output, outcome, and impact.

Let's go back to one of the user stories from Chapter 3:

 As a user of Mobile App B, I can get help from a librarian so that I can learn the right format for citing a source in my research paper, which will make my paper comply with my school's citation standard, resulting in a higher grade.

Sure enough, the story contains all three key elements:

Output: getting help from a librarian

Outcome: properly citing a source in a research paper

Impact: getting a good grade

Often, measuring the success of each output, outcome, and impact involves evaluating it from two different perspectives: the effect on your organization's external customers, and the effect on your organization's internal customers.

EXTERNAL CUSTOMERS

Let's take a look at the elements from the external customer's point of view.

Output

If you work for a university (as I did), and you've added a feature to your university's mobile app for a student to get help from a librarian, measuring the output of that should be relatively straightforward. The most logical way to measure the quantity of help would be to use web or app analytics and track the use of one or more key interactions with the help feature.

But remember that measuring the output is just the beginning of measuring success. It's the easiest thing to measure, and to some extent the least important, because a university isn't really in the business of selling library assistance. Library assistance is provided free of charge. It's a supporting service that students use to achieve other goals.

It's these other goals that you want to try to map your feature's success to. Output is certainly a milestone where you can begin your assessment, but then you need to move on to the outcome.

Outcome

Measuring the outcome of a library help feature requires more work because there isn't a simple analytics tracking code to drop into the papers of your university's students, to see whether they are now citing their sources properly.

As far as measuring this directly from students themselves, you probably need to resort to the survey method of collecting product feedback. In this case, that might entail asking a few questions about whether the library help process resulted in the student being able to write good source citations.

There are a number of ways to consider asking. You could ask a simple yes or no question, or have students rate the quality of help they received. However you decide to inquire, the extra time you invest in collecting some data about the outcome will help you tell a better story about the feature's success.

But you're still not finished. You'll also want to dig into the feature's impact.

Impact

The desired impact of the mobile app's library help feature is not to be used, or even to result in good source citations. A feature being used is nice, and having it result in proper citations is certainly laudable. But a university isn't primarily in the business of teaching students how to cite sources in research papers, either. It's in the business of having students learn and succeed academically. And the traditional way to measure such success is by students earning grades on their work.

Certainly, using a survey method could get at grade impacts of a library help feature. But the results would be considered to be pretty anecdotal. That is, students participating in the survey might have slightly rosy memories of their grades. Or, conversely, they may have been frustrated or even angry about the citation requirement. So in that case, even learning how to do citations properly may not result in them reporting on success objectively.

Because of these issues, you can see that, although you're trying to be as responsible as possible about the impact of the library help feature on students, you can't necessarily rely on students being the best source of data about that impact. Sometimes external customers themselves can't provide the best feedback.

That's where turning to internal customers can supplement the information you're seeking.

INTERNAL CUSTOMERS

As the product manager, your *primary* concern should be serving external customer needs. If your business, or your client's business, isn't focused on the customer experience, I'm not sure how you'll succeed!

Yet some needs are not articulated or measured as clearly from the customer's point of view.

 Some aspects are more behind the scenes, visible mostly to those inside the organization.

To cover the success of these aspects, it's therefore important to assess the output, outcome, and impact from the points of view of your internal customers—the people you work for directly.

Output

In the case of the library help feature, if a request can be tracked on the outbound side (from the smartphone or tablet of the person requesting assistance), it can also be measured on the inbound side (from the inbox or database that receives the request).

"Why would I bother with that?" you might wonder.

For starters, it never hurts to check both ends of a communication channel. It may be unlikely, but what if for every ten requests submitted from mobile devices, only five were received in the expected place? If you happened to discover such a problem, you just verified that something is wrong in your code, your destination e-mail address, or elsewhere.

And if you think I just made that up, think again! A team that I work with struggled for several days on exactly this issue: An outbound mobile form worked perfectly but the data didn't show up on the receiving end.

Well, the data couldn't just disappear, could it?

(As it turns out, there was a business requirement change midstream and no one told our team.)

So it might seem silly to measure simple outputs on both ends of a data transaction, but it's not funny when something changes on you and throws your feature's success under the bus. Measuring outputs both from where they're sent and where they're received isn't a bad idea.

Plus, checking with the recipients of the mobile library help requests can give you a lot of additional feedback as well. Are customers asking good questions? Are there patterns of help that are supported by the feature's design? In other words, if there are categories of help, are the categories actually used as expected or does everything come in via the "other request" option? If the latter, this observation from the internal user perspective can help influence design, too.

Again, examining the full interaction or transaction from beginning to end helps yield a more accurate picture of how successful the feature is at facilitating expected outputs.

Outcome

Remember the suggestion of surveying students about how well the library help feature supported their writing of source citations? Asking students about how effective the help is might not be the best approach, because it involves asking them to give an opinion on something that they just admitted they needed help with. So how qualified are they to evaluate the outcome of that request?

In this case, measuring the outcomes may be more complete on the internal customer side than on the external customer side, because once you start pursuing the opinions of instructors about this, you'll generally find they have more informed and experienced opinions. After all, it's their job to review the work being submitted to them (along with citations of sources).

Again, comparing feedback at both ends of the scenario is most effective. External customer satisfaction about a feature or service is part of the story, but internal customer satisfaction about the outcome is equally—if not more— important. Together, they tell a more complete story about product success.

Impact

As noted earlier, gauging the impact of a mobile library support feature might be challenging if all you do is follow up with the external customers (students). Whether through a survey, a focus group, e-mail feedback, or other means, you're really relying on subjective feedback about something that has a much more objective measure: grades. So if you can measure the impact with something more precise like grades, why not do so?

Working with sensitive customer data can be tricky in any organization, so often these types of requests take time. This is where relationship building across different roles in an organization is key to product management. Upon first meeting an instructor or department director about students' grades, your request might seem unusual. "Why is a mobile product manager meeting with me about our students' grades?" she might ask.

Use these and similar occasions to forge relationships over time and help people understand product management's role in the organization. It's easy to pigeonhole technology away from other business functions, when in fact technological solutions and business functions should be intimately connected. It's the responsibility of the product manager to correlate the outcome and impact that result from the output of customers' interactions with digital products.

NOTE **Once others in your organization see these relationships and understand how web and app solutions can truly impact customer experience as well as organizational outcomes, they won't see digital products as just the things that the design and technology teams work on.**

More people across the organization will find themselves invested in the products you work on, because reflected in them are the more specific goals they themselves are reaching toward.

So as you collect information about the output, outcome, and impact, you'll start accumulating lots of stuff: numbers, reports from analytics, anecdotal information and opinions, praise, and complaints. Should you share all of this information as you collect it, and forward e-mails to others as you receive them? No, you'll want to be deliberate about how you share it.

We'll take a closer look at how the product manager should communicate about success in the next chapter.

SUMMARY

Chapter 6 emphasized the need to keep user stories in view as new features or enhancements are completed and released to customers. User stories help set the course for the creative and technical team's work, and therefore establish ways to measure the impact of that work once it's being used by customers:

→ Review the outputs, outcomes, and impacts you established in the user stories to guide your team's work on the product. Has anything changed along the way?

→ Start with measuring the output of the site's or app's feature or service. Are people engaging with it as expected? Are your site or app analytics tracking behavior properly? If there are any concerns about how the output is being measured, correct that as soon as possible! Poor measurement of output puts the rest of your assessments at risk.

→ Once you're confident about how you're tracking the output of a feature, determine whether the output is leading to the expected outcomes. If a customer is interacting with a website or mobile app, she's doing so to answer a question or get something accomplished that relates to something that she's trying to do. Are the outputs leading to these outcomes?

→ Don't stop at measuring outcomes. What's the ultimate impact of this work? Is the website or mobile app contributing to the overall organizational strategy by increasing the sale of an item, increasing exposure to a new service, or increasing the performance or efficiency of your customers or staff?

➔ As you assess the success of your team's work, always do so by consulting internal customers as well as external customers. The opportunity for product management is to weave together the various strands of empirical and anecdotal feedback that relates to your creative and technical work, in order to tell a complete story about whether the work is delivering value to the organization.

CHAPTER 7

Communicating Product Success

After reading the previous chapter, you should have a good idea of how to measure the success of your product by using analytics and evaluating feedback from external and internal customers. But you can't simply put your effort into gathering data; you must also communicate that information effectively to the people who need to know it.

You've probably heard the mantra about getting away from your desk early and often in order to learn more about your product. The same applies to communicating about product performance: Don't let the information just sit in analytics software, spreadsheets, and e-mails. You're the messenger, and it's your job to collaborate with people throughout the learning process.

This chapter will give you some advice on how to best do this to maximize *your* outcomes and impacts as a product manager.

VISUALIZING PRODUCT DATA

Making the information about the success of your digital product readily accessible to your team and to others in your organization is an essential part of product management. If the data isn't visible, it won't attract the right kind of attention or will simply be ignored.

You can make the data about your product more compelling, however. If you can craft the reporting of your product data into a good story, people won't ignore it—they'll even ask for more.

Let's take a look at a few examples of visualizing product data.

åTracking the number of people who use your product is the starting point of web and mobile analytics. Several tools are available for this from Google, Adobe, Flurry, and others. I won't recommend any one of them or walk you through the technical side of using them. But I will share some ways of using data from any of them or another tool of your choosing.

Keeping use data visible on a regular basis will enable you—and other key people in your organization—to react quickly when you spot any curiosities or concerns in trends (**Figure 7.1**).

Here are some key details to keep in mind when you report on unique users:

→ **Use the same interval over time.** Analytics software usually allows you to play around with a variety of settings—viewing unique users by day, week, month, and so on. It can be fun to check out a variety of views and see them over different periods of time when doing your own analysis. But for communications purposes, being concise and consistent is very important.

NOTE | Edward Tufte—an expert in data visualization and information design—notes in his landmark book, *Visual Explanations*, "There are right ways and wrong ways to show data; there are displays that reveal the truth and displays that do not."[1]

Review carefully and test with others to be sure that your displays of data, especially user trends and other key metrics, are clearly understood and truthful. Part of that is keeping some variables (like time intervals) consistent in your reporting so that if someone compares it to an older report, he can draw clear and accurate conclusions.

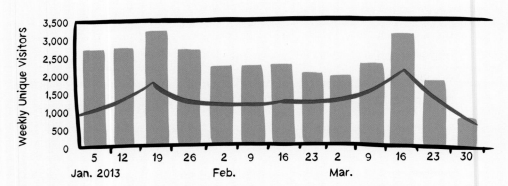

FIGURE 7.1 This graph shows weekly unique visitors over time. By overlaying them with a trend line from a previous year, the graph can clearly show whether use has changed over time.

→ **Retain important contextual data.** Context is everything. A compelling example about data context from Tufte's book is the January 1986 space shuttle Challenger disaster. NASA engineers and administrators had all of the data they needed to know that the seals between the shuttle's rockets would be compromised by the cold launch (conditions that were predicted that morning). But because of poor visual communication and a dangerous lack of context in reporting, the key data was obscured and the launch was not cancelled, resulting in disaster.[2]

In another situation (with, fortunately, less dire consequences), I was once trying to project how many of our company's customers use our mobile products. (Avoid getting into the prediction business—the value of predictions is always questionable.) My projections based solely on our own past trend data proved to be inaccurate. I was predicting a much higher adoption rate than we were getting.

Then I found data showing that other organizations were also not seeing the levels of adoption that I had been predicting. This context made my revised, lower predictions easier for others to understand. I wasn't sand-bagging the numbers to raise the odds that my predictions would be met or exceeded. I was simply providing context to show that my previous estimates were not in keeping with adoption rates in general, and our expectations should be adjusted accordingly.

Product satisfaction

Another key set of data to keep in front of your team and others in the organization is product satisfaction.

Because I work in the mobile space, one of the most convenient sources of product satisfaction data is app store ratings. I always take both the praise and the criticism with a grain of salt, of course. I assume that people who take the time to rate an app are usually one of two extremes: They are either huge fans or huge haters. (People with more moderate views often aren't motivated to rate and review.) But despite the extremes, I always hope that I'm hearing equally from both camps, so I tend to trust the average of the ratings from that source.

Still, never underestimate the value of hearing a gripe. If someone is annoyed enough about something to take a moment to write a scathing review, it's important to acknowledge it and consider what can be learned from the criticism.

With a product management mindset, you should never fear a low rating or review. Be up front about all satisfaction data with your product owners and team members. When sharing positive ratings and reviews, use the opportunity to refer back to the work that was accomplished, and lavish thanks on the many people who helped make it happen. When sharing negative ratings and reviews, use that data to highlight pain points in the product's user experience or performance. Emphasize that the bad news simply means that there's an opportunity to do something better, and tee that up as a creative and technical challenge for the team and organization to pursue (**Figure 7.2**).

App Store	Q1 2012 rating (out of 5)	Q2 2012 rating (out of 5)
Apple iTunes	3.5	3.5
Google Play	3.3	3.0
Amazon Kindle Fire	3.1	2.9
Average	3.3	3.1

FIGURE 7.2 Product ratings, particularly app store ratings that are public, can be major motivators for decisions.

However, if your product is a website, don't rule out setting up your own product satisfaction channel, similar to app store reviews. Remember the use of surveys to help determine what your minimum viable product is? You can conduct surveys that focus on product satisfaction to measure success after new enhancements or features are released to your customers. Be sure to communicate the results afterward so that others know the results.

Use by platform

If you're managing a mobile product in particular, track and report on use by device and mobile operating system type. (This is the modern equivalent of tracking which web browsers people were using in the 1990s and 2000s. Of course, this is still done today as well.)

Visualizing this type of information gives you a great excuse to insert a pie chart or two into your presentation or report. And who doesn't like a good pie chart? They're colorful, easy to understand, and usually easy to generate from the right data. I tend to make mine right in Keynote or Excel (**Figure 7.3**).

iPhone

iPad

Android smartphones

Kindle Fire tablets

Mobile Visits by Device, Jan.–Mar. 2013

FIGURE 7.3 This graph shows visits by mobile device. Pie charts make data easy to understand.

The only downside to pie charts is that they can be a little cumbersome when you're trying to show trends, such as comparing data quarter over quarter. But even then, showing two side by side can be effective.

These are, of course, just a few examples of how to visualize data. I won't exhaustively catalog the many ways to visualize by combing through every available format—you can do that on your own with Excel, PowerPoint, Keynote, and other software that generates charts and graphs.

The main takeaway here is that you want to invest the time to do these things because charts and graphs speak to people quickly, and decision makers like managers, directors, and executives are familiar with them. Visualizing data using these vehicles will get the attention of such audiences and keep it, if you make a habit of communicating with them visually week after week or quarter after quarter.

There's a lot more you can track in addition to adoption and platform with web or app analytics. Analyzing visits by content type or screen can reveal some interesting patterns of behavior. But always view such data with a critical eye, and dig in deeper as needed so you don't accidentally read too much into analytics. For example, do longer amounts of time spent in a section of your website or mobile app mean that the content is more popular and useful? Or does it just mean that there's a lot of content and it takes a while to read? Or worse yet, are customers just confused?

Principles for communicating visual data

When communicating data visually, stick to the five principles espoused by Nancy Duarte, an expert in presenting information clearly and effectively:[3]

1. Tell the truth.

2. Get to the point.

3. Pick the right tool for the job.

4. Highlight what is important.

5. Keep it simple.

WRITING PRODUCT REPORTS

In addition to sharing data and graphs about product performance, consider how you incorporate those items (and other elements) into your written communications—and the frequency with which you'll do so. This section covers some tips and techniques for writing about product outcomes and impacts.

Let's start with a short and easy one: a weekly e-mail to update people on the week's product work.

Weekly product reports

A weekly report should, in a relatively concise manner, update key people about highlights of the week.

Purpose

The goal here is to document progress wherever possible, sound any concerns as they happen to minimize surprises later, and ask key questions as they arise so you can get the information you need to keep moving ahead.

Audience

Due to its weekly frequency, you don't want to send your weekly product report to everyone in the organization (unless it's a very small organization—then it's probably OK).

Example of a weekly product report e-mail

To: Fred Olson, Mary Brown, Dylan Anderson, Laura St. John, Pat Murphy

Subject: Mobile product update - week of March 17, 2014

1. Feedback: This week we received a great comment about the new social feature in our app. "Being able to comment in the app is fantastic, and helps me feel more connected to the community. Thanks!"

2. Analytics: There was a 5 percent dip in use of the profile screen this week. I will monitor this to see whether this is a trend or an outlier. If it appears to be a trend, I'll make a note to follow up with customers about this in a future product survey or via Facebook to see if I can learn why.

3. Performance enhancement project: The performance enhancement work moved into QA testing on Wednesday, so we're on track to launch in early April.

If you have any questions or suggestions, please let me know!

Thanks,
Kris

Reference: *mobile product roadmap (PDF)*

E-mail your weekly product report to the following people:

→ Your boss

→ Project manager

→ Designer

→ Developer

→ UX analyst/designer

→ Product owner

You don't need to rigidly adhere to this list. Some products have multiple product managers, designers, developers, and other roles. Plus, if you have regular agile stand-up meetings with some team members, they might not find much value in a weekly e-mail update that repeats everything they've already heard.

The main point is to limit the scope and not inundate those higher in the organization with too much detail, too often.

Notes and recommendations

→ Focus on just three or four items. Too much information waters down the impact and raises the risk that people won't read your report.

→ Include a mix of good and bad, if possible. All good can look like there's nothing to improve (unlikely), and all bad is a downer.

→ If you have bad news to report, add a comment indicating what you'll do about it.

→ Provide a link to your roadmap document to give context for updates from week to week.

→ List recipients in to: or cc: fields so everyone knows who's involved and to encourage transparency in follow-up questions or comments.

Quarterly product reports

A quarterly report should, in a longer and more detailed way, update a broader audience about your product.

Purpose

While their purpose is similar to that of weekly reports, quarterly product reports should focus on longer trends (use and satisfaction being the most important information to share). Quarterly reports are a great opportunity to share competitive product information, comment on any significant enhancements that were released into production (or bugs that were fixed), and communicate about changes to the product roadmap.

A quarterly report can be several pages long. The longer it is, the more important it is to begin with an executive summary of key points, just in case some recipients are too busy to dive into the details.

Quarterly reports are ideally distributed via a blog, an online collaboration tool such as SharePoint or Basecamp, or a local drive—however your organization prefers to share documents. Send a link to the report via an e-mail, which should include the executive summary. Limit the executive summary to three or four main points; include the details in the full report. If you don't use document sharing services, just attach your report document to the e-mail itself.

Audience

Use quarterly product reports to communicate about your product to more people at more levels of your organization. The president or CEO should appreciate hearing about a product a few times per year, even if it's not her primary responsibility.

Share your quarterly product report with the following people:

→ Everyone on your weekly product report e-mail list

→ Design director

→ IT director

→ C-level officers, when appropriate (for example, CIO, CEO)

→ Presidents and VPs

→ Tech support/help desk director or manager

As before, there's no right answer as to whether or not a person in a specific role should receive your quarterly reports. Work with others to craft a good e-mail list, and add a disclaimer in your e-mail indicating that recipients can contact you to opt out of receiving your reports or to request that someone else be added.

Example of a quarterly product report e-mail

To: Michael McKinley, Fred Olson, Mary Brown, Dylan Anderson, Laura St. John, Pat Murphy, Susan Sommerville

Subject: Mobile Q1 2014 report

Below is a link to my Q1 2014 quarterly report about Acme Mobile.

Highlights of the mobile product report include:

- Usage and operating system trends: use increased 12%

- Updates on current work and upcoming releases: includes details on the omega feature's ongoing development

- Competitive analysis: new information about Beta Broadcasting's app

- Current view of the mobile roadmap

To download the report, click [link].

Thanks,
Kris

Notes and recommendations

→ Make quarterly reports as polished as possible, with nice graphs and other visualizations.

→ When discussing a new or enhanced feature or capability, include a screenshot or two to highlight the changes.

→ Strike a balance between reporting on product performance and product planning, which includes your performance. You want people to gain a better understanding of how the product is doing, as well as what you're currently doing to manage its ongoing success.

→ Thank others by name, especially for outstanding performance. Even if you don't manage people directly, the tone of the news in your product report can help create a positive culture where creative ideas and hard work are recognized and rewarded.

→ If you need other people or departments to help get things done, say so. Set expectations about everyone chipping in to make the organization's product a success.

COMPETITIVE ANALYSIS

Competitive analysis should always be part of your product management toolbox. The resulting document or presentation can lead to meaningful conversations about how your digital product is faring based on your own customer feedback and internal metrics, and as compared to similar products or even different approaches of your competitors.

In his book *Communicating Design*, Dan M. Brown walks through some reasons for doing competitive analysis and explains how to do it well. As he notes, you can even do meaningful competitive analysis without strictly focusing on actual competitors per se; in some cases, a *comparative* analysis—analyzing how organizations that don't compete in your market have handled similar product design problems—can be very informative.[4]

Competitor-driven analysis

A competitor-driven analysis compares the similarities and differences of your organization and your competitors. As Brown points out, competitor-driven analysis is effective at informing strategy broadly and at comparing specific features and design solutions.[5]

For example, if your digital products are e-books, a competitor-driven analysis would focus on other providers of e-books, or perhaps competitors who deliver comparable content that competes with your e-book products (in whatever format).

This analysis lets you present your product's performance in the context of your competitors' products. Do your competitors offer the same format with identical features, or do their products outperform yours in some way? Or are your competitors doing well because of other advantages, such as focusing on different subject matter, marketing differently, or simply having a slightly differ-ent market share or focus?

These are all examples of factors that could change your product's strategy, depending on how you want to differentiate yourself. Competitive analysis doesn't always result in change. It could be that, after looking more closely at how products are designed and delivered, you find that you and a competitor have very similar strategies. You might decide to continue competing quite closely. In this case, focusing on more nuanced analysis comparing specific design solutions is helpful. You both include video clips in your e-books, but how does your user experience compare with the competition's? This lets you compare approaches and use what you learn to inform your product roadmap.

Refer back to Figure 2.2, the Harvey Ball diagram in Chapter 2. Harvey Balls provide one model for communicating about your competition that helps your product team and organization's stakeholders understand the market context of their work. But there are plenty of other ways to shape competitor-driven analysis. Craft slides that compare several competitors across a tight set of criteria, showing a screenshot of each competitor's product and highlighting its strengths and weaknesses or giving numerical ratings (**Figure 7.4**).

Example of a competitive analysis slide

ACME E-BOOK CO.

CRITERIA AND ASSESSMENT

Average Amazon customer rating: 4 (out of 5)

Color illustrations: yes

Interactive illustrations: yes

Embedded audio: yes

Embedded video: no

Indexed content: yes

FIGURE 7.4 Acme e-book example.

Feature-driven analysis

Feature-driven analysis involves doing work similar to a competitor-driven analysis, but from the opposite perspective. Rather than analyzing a set of competitors across a range of features and capabilities to note similarities and differences, you set up the criteria based on features and capabilities first. (Brown also calls this a moral-driven approach.)[6]

Taking this approach is useful when you've settled on enhancing an existing feature or adding a new one. It can help you determine whether your product would be the first to include this enhancement. If you're not the first, it can help you decide how to embark on this enhancement. Are you just seeking parity with competition, or do you want to be better by designing your approach differently?

Purpose

Regardless of how you choose to analyze the competitive landscape, be aware of the risks that accompany the rewards.

By analyzing and communicating about your competition, you bring additional context to the table and bolster your team's expertise, particularly with stakeholders. More information is rarely a bad thing—you want as much context as possible to make good design decisions, consider trade-offs, and so on.

On the other hand, you don't want to lose perspective. There is a risk of people wanting to dig too far into what the competition is doing, how they're doing it, and why they're doing it. After all, you're not managing your competitors' products.

An inherent limitation of competitive analysis is that you'll rarely, if ever, know about your competitors' product strategies and roadmaps! You can't make a watertight argument about leapfrogging your competition with a particular enhancement or new feature, because that competitor might be planning the same thing at the same time. The world is full of stories about creative people in different places unknowingly "inventing" similar things at the same time. (For a fascinating example of this, look into the history of human flight—it's amazing how many separate efforts were happening concurrently in multiple countries!)

SUMMARY

This chapter highlighted the importance of communicating about product performance, both successes and challenges. Data and visualizations about product performance and satisfaction are helpful only if you facilitate good product communications:

➜ Don't settle for analytics reporting being a quiet and inconsistent practice. Instead, do it regularly and share key data in weekly and quarterly reports.

➜ Even if you analyze a wider range of product analytics, be consistent about the measures you share with others. You want people to be able to quickly compare current and previous measures, comparing apples to apples.

➜ Share a range of data that reflects customer behavior with respect to web or app content, unique users and their adoption of your product over time, and use by platform or device type.

➜ When you can, include visualizations of outcomes and impacts. Remember how good user stories include more than just outputs? So should your reports!

➜ Include competitive analysis in your reports to provide context for how your product ideas and recommendations will differentiate your organization from others. Competitive analysis can also be a source of new product ideas.

➜ Consider writing both weekly and quarterly product reports. Keep weekly ones short and sweet, and distribute them to a limited audience. Share quarterly reports to provide more in-depth detail to a wider audience.

REFERENCES

1. Tufte, Edward. 1997. *Visual Explanations*, 45. Graphics Press.

2. Tufte, 49.

3. Duarte, Nancy. 2008. *Slide:ology*, 65. O'Reilly Media.

4. Brown, Dan M. 2006. *Communicating Design*, 255. New Riders.

5. Brown, 256.

6. Brown, 256.

CHAPTER 8

Getting It Done

"We're here to put a dent in the universe. Otherwise why else even be here?"

—STEVE JOBS[1]

"Jobs's greatest creation isn't any Apple product. It is Apple itself."

—JOHN GRUBER[2]

It can be hard to start new things. Doing so requires new information, different ways of thinking about familiar ideas, and a few other things: confidence (or, to use a much more fun word, chutzpah!), focus, and the right opportunity.

You've read about how product management can help you and your team design and develop products that provide value to your customers. Now it's time to go out and, as Steve Jobs famously said, make a dent in the universe. Your product analysis and planning skills can have a positive effect on the way others interact with your products and your organization. So don't wait for an opportunity to come to you. The opportunity has arrived.

With the knowledge in this book, you can create digital products that exceed customer expectations. You can establish product management practices that help to build an organizational culture where design and development teams are trusted to take creative risks, because users routinely have the opportunity to give feedback on ideas—feedback that enables you to prioritize work and maximize results.

NOTE Most organizations have some aversion to risk. Remind your superiors that orienting your design and development efforts toward solving market problems will minimize risk. The better you understand and empathize with your customers, the better your work will align with their needs and expectations.

MAKE TIME FOR PRODUCT MANAGEMENT IN YOUR CURRENT JOB

The most important step you can take after reading this book is to put the first product management task on your calendar. After hearing this recommendation, you might ask, "When should I do this, how often, and for how long?"

If you're not a full-time product manager, I don't want to prescribe the amount and frequency of product management work that you do. To answer this for yourself, consider these questions:

→ How much longer do you want to consider setting a priority for your website or mobile app before knowing whether your users have confirmed that it's a good idea?

→ How much longer do you want to have your team designing something without knowing whether the design will solve a real problem for your customers?

→ How much longer do you want to have your team coding something before you know whether their work will improve a process, a relationship, or the bottom line for your organization?

Odds are, you don't want to be responsible for yourself or your team wasting any time at all. Time is precious, and time is money. And priorities, designs, and code are all expensive.

Regularly asking yourself these questions will help you develop a routine for gathering data from users, prototyping ideas, and analyzing your competition, so your team can move ahead with more confidence and less risk.

"International Product Management Day"

It can be a challenge even for a full-time product manager to establish a clear routine for writing user stories, prioritizing the product improvement backlog, getting in contact with users, measuring product success, and analyzing the competition. And if you're a designer or developer with other responsibilities who's trying to cover product management work, it can be harder yet.

That's because there are so many other things to do, too: stand-up meetings to attend, brainstorming and prototyping sessions to facilitate, design reviews to observe, and questions from developers, business analysts, UX designers, and others to answer. Not to mention department meetings, team meetings, and whatever else might be part of your week.

When I was being certified as a product manager, my instructor Stacey[3] told our class that to solve this problem, it's best to set aside one day per week to focus exclusively on researching market problems. Stacey calls this, somewhat tongue-in-cheek, "International Product Management Day."

If you're not a full-time product manager, it will probably be hard to get your boss to approve you spending 20 percent of your time on market-centered product management work. After all, you were hired to design, project manage, develop, or perhaps something else. So assuming this product management stuff is new to you, it's also going to be new to your supervisor. Spending one entire day per week on it? Not likely.

But don't let that dissuade you from pursuing something else that at least gets you started. How about one International Product Management Day per two-week pay period? Or maybe just one per month? Or perhaps just two or three hours per week?

However you package it, do yourself a favor and turn your noisy calendar and its incessant requests for your time into a staunch ally by regularly scheduling some focused product management time for yourself (**Figure 8.1**).

	Monday	Tuesday	Wednesday	Thursday	Friday
8 a.m.					
9					
10	Daily stand–up	Daily stand–up	Daily stand–up	Daily stand–up	Daily stand–up
	UX Review				
11					Support
Noon					
	Lunch	Gym	Lunch	Gym	Lunch
1 p.m.					
2			Int'l Product Management Day		
	Dept. Meeting			Team Meeting	
3					
4					
5					

FIGURE 8.1 Being serious about product management work means getting it on your calendar just like other important meetings and tasks.

Be sure to get your boss's approval. It shouldn't be difficult, especially if you focus on these details:

➡ Emphasize that the more often you get market data from your customers, the more information you'll have to make good product design and development decisions.

→ Note that when you show people design ideas and prototypes more often, you're less likely to waste time iterating on these ideas and refining them into more sophisticated—yet no more useful—solutions that won't actually meet expectations. Rather, you want to show people smaller amounts of progress more often, to lower design and development risk.

→ Finally, explain that the more you talk to people across your organization (your internal clients) about your web or mobile products, the better job you can do of keeping design and development tightly aligned with company strategies and initiatives.

MAKE TIME FOR PRODUCT MANAGEMENT IN SOMEONE ELSE'S JOB

Another important aspect of getting product management work done, and getting it done regularly, is not trying to do it all on your own.

So in addition to setting aside time in your own schedule, be sure to set aside time in other people's schedules as well.

 If you're a design or development manager who supervises other staff, this should be pretty easy to do. You're the boss, so you can help set parameters for how time is spent. Encourage your team members to do their own product research. Or encourage them to participate in your product management tasks.

Doing this is smart for several reasons:

→ Some tasks, like interviewing users about how they use your product and what they might want to improve, are often easier to do with two or more people, especially if you're setting up equipment to record the session. Getting assistance from others will make the work feel less burdensome and more fun.

→ Having other people on the team help with product management makes the value of the work more visible and better understood. Weekly and quarterly reports and presentations are essential, but nothing beats experiencing product management results firsthand.

→ Having other people own different product management tasks can create good karma for the team. For example, if your organization has three main competitors, you might want to have three different people on your product team (or elsewhere in your organization) be responsible for learning those competitors inside and out. Consider it a badge of honor to be the Competitor A expert.

CREATE A NEW PRODUCT MANAGEMENT POSITION FOR SOMEONE ELSE

As you get into doing the product management tasks described in this book more often, and building a culture of product management responsibility across your product team and the rest of the organization, be on the lookout for colleagues who are particularly good at helping you out. If they're great at product research, competitive analysis, interviewing or surveying customers, or analyzing data, consider making product management their primary job focus.

If you're a director or manager with the ability to create a product management position, you have an opportunity to make the tasks much more visible by designating one person as the Senior Product Manager, Product Manager, or Associate Product Manager, depending on her level of experience.

Write a product manager job description

Of course, if you decide to add a product manager to your organization or team (especially from outside the organization, which means you need to recruit and interview candidates), you have to be able to describe what they do. You may want to highlight the tasks described in this book as part of a job description.

But aside from the details, how do you capture the overall responsibility and expectations of a product manager? To help you with that, I've written a sample job description for a product manager at the fictitious Acme Digital Corporation.

Like any job description, a product manager job description will vary from company to company and even product to product. So don't take this sample as gospel. Rather, use it to help you

➜ Emphasize that being a product manager is a people-focused job that requires empathy with customer and market problems.

➜ Find candidates who are comfortable with user experience design even though it's a somewhat nebulous field, and preferably who have both creative and technical backgrounds in addition to some practical management experience.

➜ Identify people who are good at getting things done and communicating the results of their work.

Sample Job Description

At Acme Digital, we put our customers first. From functional websites to tightly engineered mobile applications, we design and build products that help people and their families organize their priorities and manage their busy lives.

The product management team works closely with designers and developers to guide products from conception to launch. As part of the company's product management team, you will bridge the technical and business worlds as you design solutions that our customers love. You'll work with people from engineering, corporate communications, marketing, and finance. We are looking for an independent self-starter who enjoys identifying problems and breaking them down into steps that help drive product design and development.

Responsibilities:

1. Work with the user experience and technical support departments to identify opportunities to improve our web and mobile products.

2. Write user stories, prioritize the product backlog, and help gather business requirements.

3. Define a product's business vision and strategy by working with executives, directors, and managers to align digital product planning with business goals and to identify metrics that will validate product success.

Qualifications:

1. Product management, design, or development experience with a focus on digital products and web technology.

CREATE OR FIND A NEW PRODUCT MANAGEMENT POSITION FOR YOURSELF

When I was first thinking about writing this book, I wanted to make it useful for a target audience who might be like me. I originally got into website and mobile app development primarily via marketing and design. And as I advanced—especially when I wanted to formally immerse myself in the knowledge and culture of the academic study of design—I eventually found myself in a master of fine arts program in interactive design.

What's interesting, though, is that some of the most important things I've learned about design and development weren't learned in graduate school. In fact, they weren't learned during web conferences either (gasp!).

Many of the most important things I've learned along the way have been the insights I've gained in usability labs or via customer surveys, as I've observed how regular people interact with websites and mobile apps. And, better yet, when I've had the chance to meet with customers and listen to what they have to say.

This has meant, somewhat ironically, that getting away from other designers and developers—and increasing my time spent talking about web and mobile technology with people who are not just like me—has resulted in some of the best product ideas and insights. And sometimes these conversations have had nothing to do with the projects I've worked on.

Rather, it's the conversations about smartphones and apps that I've had on the sidelines of my daughters' soccer games that have yielded some of the best design insights—just talking to everyday people about everyday challenges, and how web and mobile technologies might do a better job tomorrow than they do today.

I certainly don't regret any of my career choices along the way to becoming a digital product manager. But I do wish I'd known more about what being a product manager was before I actually had the job title. Because, in hindsight, I'd been doing product management work for a few years before I ever had the words "product manager" on my business card. But I didn't know how to do it better until I was more aware of what I was doing, and was working as a product manager.

> **NOTE** | **If you're the type of designer or developer who likes to follow orders, execute your work efficiently and in a solid fashion, and wipe your hands afterwards, you may want to keep doing what you're doing for a while longer. You can stay focused on what you love doing, and continue working in that capacity. There's nothing wrong with that at all.**

So if you find yourself thinking about why you're designing what you're asked to design, or you're not sure whether you should be developing a particular solution if you have another one in mind, product management might be for you. If this is the case, be confident about asking questions rather than continuing to follow orders.

Also, start doing research about what you're asked to do. Offer up alternatives. Tell someone that she might not really want Option A—ask if she's considered Option B or C.

If you're ready to expand your definitions of craft and creativity into the delightfully messy work of spending time with a wide variety of people, from customers to executives, identifying new opportunities to design and develop new or better solutions, you're ready to dig into product management.

If so, I hope this book helps get you started. Good luck, and stay in touch![4]

SUMMARY

Chapter 8 helped you start integrating product management into your organization:

→ Don't expect product management tasks to happen on their own. Set aside time on your calendar for product management and use it for what it's intended—no playing solitaire or checking your social networks allowed!

→ Help others on your product team or in your organization do the same thing. Invite them to help you out with your work if you're leading product management work, or if you supervise people then use the opportunity to assign product management tasks to them.

→ Hire people to do product management work by making sure that you're describing the work as a broad range of responsibilities from design to writing and analysis.

→ Create a product-oriented culture so that everyone, no matter what their role, is interested in and exposed to people who use your websites and mobile apps. Expose them to the business side of your organization as well. Encourage research and new ways of thinking so that product management can be a source of ideas and strategic direction.

REFERENCES

1. Snell, Jason. "Steve Jobs: Making a Dent in the Universe." *Macworld*. http://www.macworld.com/article/1162827/steve_jobs_making_a_dent_in_the_universe.html.

2. Gruber, John. "Resigned." *Daring Fireball*. http://daringfireball.net/2011/08/resigned.

3. Stacey Weber works as an instructor for Pragmatic Marketing, an education company that trains and certifies product managers. You can find more information at www.pragmaticmarketing.com.

4. You can contact me via my website, www.kristoferlayon.com. Don't hesitate to ask a question or share your own product management stories and successes by proposing a guest blog post. I look forward to hearing from you!

APPENDIX

Product Design Research

In Chapter 4, "Analyzing and Prioritizing Enhancements," I referred to *Universal Methods of Design,* Bella Martin and Bruce Hanington's excellent book about product design research, which highlights 100 approaches to researching product problems, ideas, and solutions. I've used several of the ideas described in the book in my own design and management work over the years. Here are a few that I'd recommend most.

A/B TESTING

Say you're in an early product design analysis phase and your team has proto-typed two seemingly good ideas. Or it's later in the design process and you've settled on the next priority, but haven't found a clear design path forward.

If you're fretting over how to break a tie between two solutions that seem equal, put the ideas or prototypes directly in front of your customers and see which one most effectively meets or exceeds their needs. This is called A/B testing.[1]

If the feature isn't too expensive to fully design and develop, consider com-pleting two versions of it and putting them both into production. You might even consider finding a way to send 50 percent of your users to one version of the solution and 50 percent to the other. (Google is well known for this kind of A/B testing.) Or put one version up for a week or two, then replace it with the other if you don't want to send customers to two different places at once.

A/B testing can provide additional perspective about which option to imple-ment. But it may not necessarily answer why one is better than the other, so don't hesitate to follow up A/B testing with additional inquiry.

HEURISTIC EVALUATION

Heuristic evaluation is a usability research method in which professional evaluators review a product to determine how well it complies with generally accepted user interface design principles.[2] This is best done as a prerequisite to usability testing with customers. That way, what you're taking the time to test with others has already been deemed to meet an acceptable standard of usability.

Martin and Hanington base their ten heuristic principles on a seminal article about usability testing written by Jakob Nielsen in 1995:[3]

1. Visibility of system status: Inform or update users about processes that are happening in a way that's timely and easy to understand.

2. Match between system and the real world: Use natural language and labeling instead of more obscure, system-based terminology. In short, communicate with people on their terms.

3. User control and freedom: Design the experience in a way that affirms that the user is in control. In particular, make the workflow easy to understand and include steps that are easy to trace forward and backward in the process.

4. Consistency and standards: Don't use different words for the same thing, or the same word for different things. Use clear and consistent language to minimize the likelihood of confusion.

5. Error prevention: If there's a possibility of "user error," take that into account and minimize the odds of errors happening.

6. Recognition rather than recall: Make details, instructions, and options visible and easy to return to. Hiding away something important forces the user to remember where it is or, worse yet, to hunt for it again.

7. Flexibility and efficiency of use: Customize or expedite product use for repeat or advanced users.

8. Aesthetic and minimalist design: Avoid making things more elaborate than necessary, whether in content or design detail.

9. Help users recognize, diagnose, and recover from errors: Use clear and natural language to confirm an error situation and explain to the user what to do next.

10. Help and documentation: The best designs need little to no documentation. But for more complex products, documentation is sometimes unavoidable. Make any support information easy to find, use simple language, and break it down into bite-sized steps.

PERSONAS

As you collect information about your customers, look for patterns that emerge. If you notice some things that are common among your customers, consider using those traits to describe your typical customer (or customers) in terms of personas.[4]

The goal of a persona is to represent a typical customer in one page of information—a concise snapshot depicting who he or she is. You typically want to make the person seem as real as possible, so including essential information like gender, age, and other personal information is a good start. Depicting each persona with a photo (hopefully something that looks more natural than a stock image) can help make the persona real.

Include as much information as possible about the persona's goals, tasks, or needs, and when things need to be done during lengthier processes. For example, if the persona is a student, what tasks are important to her and when do they happen?

Personas should never replace interacting with real customers as often as possible. But in between such interactions, having personas visible to the team and referring to them can help reinforce a customer-centric state of mind when planning, designing, and developing digital product solutions.

SHADOWING

Shadowing sounds pretty fun, like something out of a James Bond film. But I'm not recommending that you secretly stalk customers to see what they do. Shadowing isn't covert! It's about quietly observing a customer for an extended period of time during a typical day in her life. It's a time-consuming approach, but it's well worth it.[5]

Consider the main advantage of shadowing someone. It's you, not her, who is more inconvenienced. This gives the customer a more typical experience, except for the fact that you're observing—again, being quiet and unobtrusive is key here. It also allows you to usability test something in a more natural environment than a usability lab or your company's office.

So if you really want to see how a website or mobile app performs, consider shadowing someone about once a month, or however often you can make the time to do so. Take notes and even record her if she gives you permission. What you observe should be much more than her product interactions and outcomes. Pay attention to her environment (physical, personal, and whatever else impacts her time and attention). Also make note of her mood. Was she successful but not happy? Lots of small details can add up to a lot of product knowledge for you later.

USER JOURNEY MAP

A user journey map is a comprehensive document covering information learned from all of these methods outlined above and more. It's most often a visual document, though it can start with a more hands-on method of using sticky notes on a whiteboard or wall to get it going.[6]

The premise of a user journey map is that a user has a series of goals she's trying to achieve when encountering an organization and its products. Stepping back from existing or planned products, what are these goals? And what is their sequence?

A good user journey map is a living document that accrues more detail over time. So let's say you shadow someone and learn something interesting about what she was trying to accomplish during her day. If this detail relates to your current or future product offering in any way, be sure to document that detail on your user journey map.

Referring to user journey maps during product planning and design can help your team stay focused on solving user stories, as user stories should tie back to processes illustrated in the user journey map.

REFERENCES

1. Martin and Hanington, 8.

2. Martin and Hanington, 99.

3. Nielsen, Jakob. "10 Usability Heuristics for User Interface Design." http://www.nngroup.com/articles/ten-usability-heuristics/.

4. Martin and Hanington, 132.

5. Martin and Hanington, 158.

6. Martin and Hanington, 196.

INDEX

attribute-level hierarchies, 58–63
levels of needs, 55–57, 59–61
overview, 53–54
product-level hierarchies, 57–58

I

informal prototyping, 85–87
innovation requirements, 142
in-person usability testing, 96–97
Interactive Project Management, 10
internal customers
defining customers, 28–29
measuring product success, 108–112

J

job descriptions, product management, 148–150
Jobs, Steve, 141–142
journey maps, 163

K

Kano, Noriaki, 64–75
Kano model for prioritization, 64–65
attributes
applying, 66–73
basic, 65
delightful, 66
performance, 65
visualizing, 73–76
Keynote for data charts, 123
Krug, Steve, 30, 99

L

lab-based usability testing, 98

Lean, 82
Lyons, Nancy, 10–11

M

markets
customers
A/B testing, 158
defining value, 23–24
external, 29–30
internal, 28–29
persona development, 161
shadowing, 162
user stories, 36–47
and demand, 20–22
problems
focus on, 30–31, 144
user stories, 36–47
and supply, 24–27
Martin, Bella, 75, 157
Maslow, Abraham, 53–60
Maslow, human needs and prioritization
application to mobile user experiences, 59–63
hierarchies
attribute-level, 58–63
product-level, 57–58
levels of needs, 55–57, 59–61
overview, 53–54
measuring product success
customers
A/B testing, 158
external, 106–108
internal, 108–112
persona development, 161
shadowing, 162
user stories, 105–106
web and mobile analytics, 104
milestones, 83

minimum viable product. *See* MVP
MVP (minimum viable product), 83–84
definitions
of minimum, 83
of viable, 84
features
partially built, 89
released, 89–90
feedback, 90
card sorting, 94–96
informal talks with users, 91–92
usability testing, heuristic methods, 159–160
usability testing, in-person, 96–97
usability testing, lab-based, 98
usability testing, online, 97
user surveys, 92–93
internal milestones, 83
prototyping
A/B testing, 158
formal, 88
informal, 85–87
paper, 86–87
whiteboarding, 84–85

N

Nielsen, Jakob, 159

O

online usability testing, 97

P

paper prototyping, 86–87
persona development, 161
physiological needs, 55–56, 59–60

KRISTOFER LAYON (author) started designing for the desktop web in 1996, and moved into designing user experiences and products for smartphones and tablets in 2009. Kris currently leads product management and UX design for Red Stamp, a mobile-first social commerce company. You can learn more about him at *www.kristoferlayon.com*.

WHITNEY HESS (foreword) coaches senior leaders and product teams on how to cultivate compassion for customers and colleagues. Her life's mission is to put humanity back into business. Whitney is the founder and principal of the user experience consultancy Vicarious Partners, and the author of the *Pleasure & Pain* blog at *www.whitneyhess.com/blog*.

ADAM TURMAN (illustrator) has been designing, illustrating, and screen-printing since 2003. He's worked with Kris for several years on the popular art prints for MinneWebCon, Minnesota's Web Conference. You can see more of Adam's work at *www.adamturman.com*.

The body text is set in Whitney, originally developed in 1996 by Tobias Frere-Jones for the Whitney Museum of American Art in New York City. Headings are set in Trade Gothic, designed in 1948 by Jackson Burke at Linotype. Illustrations use Turman Grotesk, designed by Adam Turman and Chank Diesel.